Quickies Morning, Noon and Night

Denise Fletcher

Marshall Cavendish Cuisine

Editor: Sylvy Soh Hui Ling
Designer: Rachel Chen Choon Jet
Photographer: Joshua Tan, Elements by the Box

Published by Marshall Cavendish Cuisine
An imprint of Marshall Cavendish International
1 New Industrial Road, Singapore 536196

Other Marshall Cavendish Offices:
Marshall Cavendish Ltd.5th Floor, 32–38 Saffron Hill, London EC1N 8FH • Marshall Cavendish Corporation. 99 White Plains Road, Tarrytown NY 10591-9001, USA • Marshall Cavendish International (Thailand) Co Ltd. 253 Asoke, 12th Flr, Sukhumvit 21 Road, Klongtoey Nua, Wattana, Bangkok 10110, Thailand • Marshall Cavendish (Malaysia) Sdn Bhd, Times Subang, Lot 46, Subang Hi-Tech Industrial Park, Batu Tiga, 40000 Shah Alam, Selangor Darul Ehsan, Malaysia

National Library Board Singapore Cataloguing in Publication Data

Fletcher, Denise
Quickies : morning, noon and night / Denise Fletcher. Singapore : Marshall Cavendish Cuisine, c2009.
p. cm.
ISBN-13 : 978-981-261-849-8
ISBN-10 : 981-261-849-X

1. Quick and easy cookery. I. Title.

TX833.5
641.555 -- dc22 OCN298770595

Printed in Singapore by KWF Printing Pte Ltd

Dedication

I wish to thank the following people:

My grandmother, for teaching my mother to cook to the best of her ability, in spite of abject and heart breaking poverty.

My mother, for her strength and her faith.

My husband, for being my rock and my water.

JP, JJ, JC–for being you.

My Command Cabin buddies, Suzi, Susi, Lele and my evil twin M for their priceless friendship and for taking me "places" I never thought I'd go. **Wink**.

Anyone who took the time to pick my book off the shelf and buy it. I hope you don't regret it. **Crossing fingers**.

Last, but not least, my editor, designer, photographer and publisher, for making this a reality. I'm still pinching myself.

Contents

Introduction

I began writing down recipes in October 2004, hoping that they would somehow morph into a cookbook. It eventually hit me that the only way I would achieve my goal would be by keeping a personal food journal. Therefore, I would cook something, and if I really liked it, the recipe would be photographed and recorded. Such has been the genesis of this cookbook. My husband, who inspired the title, has always appreciated the sensuousness of food. Food is a wonderful way to bring people closer, and I dedicate my cookbook to couples everywhere and to the undeniable pleasures of the table. I urge you to cook for, and feed each other as often as you can. It has done wonders for my relationship; I hope it will do the same for yours.

Having said that, there is no real reason why everybody else can't enjoy the recipes here (no booze for the kiddies though!). They are delectable, easy and quick and in this day of "I want that ready yesterday", who doesn't want "delectable, easy and quick"? Most of the recipes will feed 2–4 but can easily be halved or doubled to feed almost any number of people.

As a chef, I was formally trained in the classical French tradition and have several years of field experience as well. However, I understand that not everyone who picks up this book will have the same training and experience. Thus, I have ensured that every recipe in this book gives good results without the need for fancy equipment or complicated, time-consuming techniques. My recipes are geared toward speed and convenience to suit today's hectic lifestyle. Measurements may be in the metric system or cups, depending on which is more convenient for the recipe at hand. And if I can't find a certain ingredient, I will substitute it without hesitation. I have never believed in being chained to tradition, and I will always believe that the proof of the pudding is in the eating. I have a home and family to see to, without a domestic helper, and varied interests I am determined to pursue. I understand only too well the pressures and demands of modern life. Hence, I have honed my recipes to make them easier, faster, yet every bit as delicious as they would be had you spent hours in the kitchen.

The recipes are not divided into courses, but are, as suggested by the book's title, loosely grouped into things that you might want to eat in the morning, afternoon or at night. I have also included chapters for desserts, baked goods and drinks. My sections on kitchen tips, wine and coffee were written to address the thirst for knowledge and burgeoning interest these two complex yet bewitching subjects have aroused. Most of the recipes are my creations, and a few are time-tested classics. The recipes are eclectic, because I am of Portuguese, English and Asian descent, and I am too curious about global cuisine to ever be satisfied eating only one type of food. In our home, no one is sure what we'll be having for lunch or dinner on any given day, and I suppose it's only natural that some of that element of surprise would creep into the pages of this book.

I think it's quite tragic that in many homes today, the kitchen has become merely an expensive showcase, fitted with every imaginable appliance, all in gleaming steel and begging to be used, but left mostly untouched, except for toasting frozen pizza or boiling water for a cup of tea. I hope that apart from finding quick, easy and satisfying eating options in this cookbook, you will also find pleasure, a bit of fun, and a reprieve from the frenzied and frenetic reality that life can sometimes be. May this cookbook be a feast for your senses, a guide rather than an instruction manual, and proof that you can easily and pleasurably cook and eat well in your own kitchen.

Happy cooking and happier eating!

Love,

Denise

Basic Kitchen Equipment

In the two decades that I've been cooking, I've found that despite having two large drawers full of gadgets, I keep going back to the same basic equipment. There are certainly loads of other things that are nice to have, like food processors or espresso machines, but the following items are all you truly need, if you're going to make a habit of cooking at home and intend to do it with speed, enjoyment and economy.

Chef's Knife

Also known as a cook's knife or French knife. It's built for slicing, dicing, mincing, chopping and almost any cutting job in the kitchen. A chef's knife always has a curved blade which allows fast and precise cutting, due to its ability to rock back and forth on the cutting board. Chef's knives come in a range of sizes, the most common being about 20 cm for the blade's length. Get a larger size for more versatility.

Bread/Serrated Knife

This makes for effortless cutting through thick-skinned foods, such as tomatoes, capsicums and crusty bread to produce neat and clean slices. To maintain the sharpness of the cutting edges, never cut bones or other hard things with it, and always do cutting on a board. Actually, this applies for most knives except bone saws. You do, however, need to take extra care with a serrated knife as it is much harder to sharpen than a straight-edged knife.

Paring Knife

This is really a scaled-down chef's knife, but is designed to be a multi-tasker, and is able to handle much finer work. It is perfect for peeling onions, garlic, fruit and vegetables that are awkward for the vegetable peeler. And if you want to take your food presentation up a notch, it's also handy for intricate tasks such as cutting avocado and mango fans, or radish and tomato roses.

Chinese Cleaver

This comes in several sizes but cleavers are generally large, heavy knives with a broad blade. Good for cutting through small and medium bones and joints, slicing, chopping, dicing and mincing, flattening and tenderizing chops and steaks, skinning garlic and small onions super quick and even sliding whole cakes onto serving platters. The best ones are made from a single piece of high carbon steel, which sharpens well but tends to rust. This can be countered by thoroughly drying the blade after washing and before storing. Although stainless steel blades are rust-resistant, they are not as strong as carbon steel, and cannot maintain a sharp edge as long as a carbon steel knife can. When storing, keep knives separate from each other in a knife block or attached to a magnetic strip; don't dump them together in a drawer as they will blunt each other's cutting edges.

Vegetable Peeler

I have only one vegetable peeler. It's made entirely of stainless steel and shaped like a catapult, very ergonomic and supremely comfortable to use. It costs $15.90 but is worth every cent, as it glides through everything like hot steel through butter. It is also excellent for making cucumber/zucchini/carrot/radish ribbons and Parmesan cheese shavings. Plus, it's absolutely gorgeous–the real reason I bought it.

Wine Opener

I like the double lever corkscrew. It has two "arms" or levers and a screw head. Holding the bottle securely with one hand, insert the tip of the corkscrew into the centre of the cork and turn the screw head until it sinks into the cork. As you turn the screw head, the levers will rise up. To remove the cork, push the levers all the way down. This will cause the cork to be pulled out of the bottle. Just give a tug and the cork comes completely out.

What to do when the cork crumbles and falls into the wine while you're trying to uncork the bottle? Very aggravating but hardly the end of the world. If the entire cork has fallen in, your best bet is to pour the wine out through a tea strainer into wine glasses or a wine decanter if you have one. If the cork keeps getting stuck in the neck of the bottle as you're pouring, push it out of the way with a chopstick inserted into the bottle as you pour. If the cork has partially broken off and a chunk of it remains in the neck of the bottle, your corkscrew won't help. Push the cork all the way into the bottle using a sturdy chopstick and yes, get out your tea strainer.

Other Stuff

Three chopping boards Generously-sized, able to fit in your sink, wooden or plastic

Chinese cast-iron wok Cast from a single piece of metal or with riveted handles.

Large deep pot For boiling pasta

A steel fryer

A steel fish slice

A deep bowled Chinese stock ladle

A pair of steel kitchen tongs

Cast iron or blue steel, flat-bottomed frying pan
Blue steel is a specially treated high carbon content steel that has the same characteristics and requires the same care as cast iron but is more durable. I highly recommend it. When new, follow seasoning instructions. After each use, clean with hot water and an abrasive sponge if necessary, using no soap. Dry immediately and thoroughly before keeping. I heat it on the stove until completely dry. With repeated use and proper care, it will develop a patina that will render it naturally non-stick.

Tiered steamer At least 2 steaming layers, steel or bamboo

A granite pestle and mortar

A can opener

Electricals

Blender

Oven

Toaster oven

Microwave oven Really handy if you're in a hurry, but not essential.

Baking

One 23 cm round cake tin

One 23 cm square cake tin

One 10 cm by 23 cm loaf tin

Two 6-cup deep muffin tins

Two cookie sheets

One 18 cm by 28 cm brownie tin

One 23 cm by 35 cm Swiss roll tin

One medium-sized balloon whisk (ensure it's comfy in your hand!)

One thin flexible rubber spatula/scraper

Two pastry brushes

One kitchen scale Clearly calibrated in 10 g or 20 g graduation.

Two steel mixing bowls

The cooking equipment list may seem scanty, but I've been using exactly what you see above in all my cooking since 1998, when the last of my "chef-quality sandwich bottom designer" cookware passed on to the hereafter. Shopping for kitchen gadgets and equipment is fun. If you see something you really like, add it to your kitchen arsenal. We all have our weaknesses and you really can't have too many shoes or coffee makers, my personal (kitchen) fetish.

For your Pantry

Oils

Extra virgin olive oil For dressings and flavouring food.

Pure olive oil If you do a lot of Mediterranean cooking.

Sunflower, soy bean or peanut oil For Asian cooking.

Toasted sesame seed oil As a flavour accent for Asian cooking.

Flavourings and Seasonings

Canned coconut milk

Chinese cooking wine

Dry white vermouth

Dark soy sauce

Light soy sauce

Oyster sauce

Sesame seeds Both black and white varieties.

Thai fish sauce Refrigerate once opened.

White vinegar

Your favourite liqueurs

Herbs and Spices

Black pepper seeds

Cardamom pods

Cinnamon sticks

Chilli flakes

Cumin seeds

Garlic

Dried oregano or marjoram The only dried herbs worth buying. Use fresh herbs whenever possible.

Onions

White pepper seeds

Whole cloves

Good To Have

Anchovies Bottled, canned or in a tube.

Bottled salted capers Dry salted flower buds of a Mediterranean shrub. Smaller capers are better. Available preserved in brine or dry salted. Dry salted is preferable. Italian capers are best.

Black and green olives

Italian tomato paste Try to get this in tube form–much more convenient.

Starches

Angel hair pasta or capellini Very fine spaghetti which cooks in 2 minutes.

Bucattini Tubular spaghetti.

Penne rigate Angled ribbed macaroni.

Spaghetti

Basmati rice

Couscous Tiny wheat pellets very similar to semolina (sugee). A North African staple.

Fragrant Thai rice

Polenta Coarse ground corn.

Rolled oats

Split red lentils Cooks tender in 20 minutes only.

For Your Refrigerator

Dairy

Butter

Dairy cream

Milk

Yoghurt

Sour cream or crème fraîche See page 159.

Seasonings and Condiments

Dijon mustard

Powdered English mustard

Prepared wasabi paste

Salted black bean paste

Fresh Herbs, Spices and Vegetables

Chillies Red, green and the bird's eye variety.

Coriander (cilantro) leaves

Ginger

Lemons

Lemon grass

Limes Calamansis or large green limes.

Parsley

Screwpine leaves

Tomatoes I like Italian Roma tomatoes for their firm flesh, sweet taste and fewer seeds.

Miscellaneous

Baking soda

Cream of tartar

Dark chocolate Valrhona/Lindt/Droste/Ritter Sport or any European brand with at least 50% cocoa solids. In a pinch, good quality cocoa powder will do far better than inferior chocolate, dark or otherwise.

Instant yeast granules

Plain (all-purpose) flour For cakes, biscuits, cookies, pastry, thickening sauces.

Pure cocoa powder

Pure ground coffee Look for 100% Arabica bean coffee regardless of brand or origin. Refer to chapter Kitchen Smarts (page 161) for more information.

Vanilla extract

Whole almonds

Conversion Tables

Amount	Grams	Millilitres	Spoons	Ounces	Pounds
1 teaspoon	6 g	5 ml			
1 tablespoon	18 g	15 ml	3 tsp		
1 cup	100 g	200 ml	12 Tbsp	4 oz 8 fl oz	
1 kilogram	1000 g				2 lb 4 oz
1 pound	454 g			16 oz	
1 ounce	28 g	25 ml	1½ Tbsp		
1 litre		1000 ml		36 fl oz	

tsp = teaspoon	Tbsp = tablespoon	kg = kilogram	ml = millilitre
oz = ounce	lb = pound	g = gram	l = litre

I realise that the amounts don't exactly add up proportionately in every case. My measurements are based on convenience and practicality rather than mathematical accuracy. Don't worry, you'll quickly get the hang of approximation and once you do, you'll find cooking so much more enjoyable.

Oven Description	Gas Mark	Temperature (°C)	Temperature (°F)
Cool	1	140°C	280°F
	2	150°C	300°F
Warm	3	160°C	325°F
Moderate	4	180°C	350°F
Moderately Hot	5	190°C	370°F
	6	200°C	400°F
Hot	7	210°C	410°F
Very Hot	8	220°C	440°F
	9	230°C	450°F

Morning

Not a morning person? Didn't the doctor and your mother tell you that breakfast is the most important meal of the day? Other than for an energy boost to kickstart your day, breakfast is very essential, in more ways than you can imagine. Get your chocolate and caffeine fix, all in one sinfully delicious Sticky Chocolate Nut Coffeecake. Chase away the booze demons the morning after a big night out with a Hangover Sandwich. Whip up a Languid Sunday Brunch for the family on a lazy weekend, and share a Breakfast in Bed Frittata with that someone special... in bed, of course.

A frittata is an Italian open-faced omelette that's cooked in a pan and finished off in the oven. This is easy, very tasty and uses ingredients that most people would have in their kitchen. Serve with lots of crusty baguette, fried tomatoes and steaming coffee. Now, take your plate, slip back under the covers, turn on the telly and wrest the remote away from resident channel surfing junkie. Thank God for weekends!

Breakfast in Bed Frittata

Olive or vegetable oil 3 Tbsp

Black pitted olives 5, sliced

Green pitted olives 5, sliced

Large onion, 1, peeled and thickly sliced

Ham 2 slices, thickly sliced or diced

Sausages of any variety 3, thickly sliced

Canned tomato sauce 4 Tbsp

Salt ½ levelled tsp

Grated Parmesan cheese ½ cup

Grated Gouda cheese ½ cup

Freshly ground black pepper to taste

Dried mixed Italian herbs a fat pinch

Large eggs 6, beaten, in a large bowl

- Preheat oven at 180°C.
- Heat oil in a pan with an ovenproof handle and when really hot, add in olives, onion, ham and sausage. Stir over high heat for about 2 minutes, then add tomato sauce and salt. Stir, then reduce heat.
- Add cheeses, pepper and herbs to the beaten eggs in the bowl. Stir lightly then pour mixture into pan. Shake pan slightly to distribute egg. When omelette is partially set, slide pan into oven and bake for about 10 minutes or until eggs are sufficiently set to cut into wedges. Do not overcook.
- Remove from oven and cool 5 minutes before cutting into wedges.

To Prepare: **10 minutes** To Cook: **15 minutes** Serves: **2–4**

Breakfast made for two

I love oats but hate porridge, so muesli it is. Just add cold milk to the oats, flavour according to whim, stir and eat. Here I used nearly everything I had in the kitchen but the sink. Seriously though, my combination of dried pineapple, papaya, cranberries, sultanas, fresh raspberries and almonds add up to a gorgeous clash of colour, flavour and texture. A sprinkle of sweet spice makes it even more interesting and a slur of thick, cold cream turns this into a healthy treat that's just a bit more indulgent. Did I mention that both oats and cinnamon are supposed aphrodisiacs? Double whammy anyone?

Kitchen Sink Muesli

Fine rolled oats 6 levelled Tbsp

Salt a pinch or to taste

Cold milk as much or as little as you like

Dried or fresh fruits of choice 1 generous handful or to taste

Coarsely chopped toasted nuts of choice 2 Tbsp or to taste

Ground cinnamon ½ levelled tsp

Thick cold cream (optional) 1–2 Tbsp

Sugar (optional) to taste

- Put oats into a bowl, add salt and pour milk over. Stir and leave to soak for about 3 minutes.
- Sprinkle with fruits and nuts of choice and cinnamon. Add cream and sugar if you wish. If you're using a generous amount of dried fruit, you may not need any sugar.
- Stir and eat.

To Prepare: **5 minutes** Serves: **1**

A savoury twist on the Sticky Chocolate and Nut Coffeecake (see page 33). This is an easy way to impress guests if you're doing brunch and is also good as picnic fare. I used a mixture of onion, olives and tuna which is somewhat Mediterranean but you really can use whatever you like–ham, bacon, tomatoes, mushrooms, peppers, anchovies, artichoke hearts or smoked salmon to name a few. Pretty much anything you fancy would fit right in.

Savoury Breakfast Quick Bread

Plain (all-purpose) flour 1¼ cups

Baking soda ½ levelled tsp

Cream of tartar 1 levelled tsp

Instant yeast granules 1 levelled tsp

Garlic powder ½ levelled tsp

Dried mixed Italian herbs ½ levelled tsp

Ground white pepper ¼ levelled tsp

Salt ¼ levelled tsp

Egg 1

Buttermilk or plain yoghurt ¼ cup

Water ⅓ cup

Grated sharp Cheddar or Gouda cheese 1 cup

Onion ½, peeled, cut into thick rings and lightly fried

Black pitted olives 6, thickly sliced

Green pitted olives 6, thickly sliced

Red bell pepper (capsicum) ½, cored and cut into small dice

Canned tuna 1 tin, drained and flaked

Olive oil sufficient for drizzling

- Set oven at 180°C and grease a 20-cm by 30-cm baking tray.
- Thoroughly combine the flour, baking soda and cream of tartar in a large bowl. Add yeast, garlic powder, herbs, pepper and salt and stir until very well mixed.
- Add egg, buttermilk and water to the dry ingredients and stir with a whisk until smooth and yeast grains have dissolved. Add half the grated cheese and stir gently to mix.
- Pour batter into tray.
- Scatter the onion rings, olives, bell pepper, tuna and remaining cheese evenly over the top of batter. Drizzle with a little olive oil and bake for 20 minutes. Remove from oven and cool for 5 minutes before cutting into 8 or 12 pieces. Serve warm.

To Prepare: **10 minutes** To Bake: **20 minutes** Serves: **4**

Hang that hangover!

This sandwich saved me once, in my youthful folly. It's good in its own right but really does taste its best when you're grappling with a monster hangover. If you like peanut butter, you will love this. The peanut butter provides the rich and savoury base note while the tangy jam and fresh fruit give it a bracing lift. What I really love is the contrast between the crunchy-as-glass crust and the warm, tender and oozing interior.

Hangover Sandwich

White or wholemeal sandwich bread 8 slices

Peanut butter preferred amount

Strawberry jam preferred amount

Eggs 2

Vanilla extract ½ tsp

Sugar 1 tsp

Vegetable oil ½ cup

Icing (confectioner's) sugar sufficient for dusting

Cinnamon powder ½ tsp

Ripe strawberries 8, washed, hulled, drain and cut as you like

Golden Delicious apples 2, small, cored and cut as you like, or use any variety of apples

Seedless oranges 2, small, skinned and cut up as you like

- Make your peanut butter and jam sandwiches as you normally would. Don't use too much peanut butter and jam or you will make a mess when you cut the fried sandwiches. Keep the outer edges clean so they don't burn when you fry them.
- Beat the eggs in a soup plate with the vanilla and sugar. Heat oil in a frying pan.
- When moderately hot, dip two sandwiches, one at a time into the egg mixture, shake off excess and put into hot oil. Fry each side for about 2 minutes. Turn often to prevent scorching.
- Drain sandwiches on kitchen paper and repeat with the other 2 sandwiches. Cool slightly before cutting.
- Cut sandwiches into triangles and dust with icing sugar and a little cinnamon. Serve on individual plates with cut strawberries, apples and oranges on the side. Don't forget the coffee.

To Prepare: **10 minutes** To Cook: **8 minutes** Serves: **4**

This is beautiful, absolutely scrumptious and incredibly easy. Portobello mushrooms are best but Swiss brown mushrooms or fresh shiitake will do too. If fresh basil varieties are unavailable, use a mix of your favourite salad greens. The dressing is simplicity in itself and wonderfully fresh and intense. Serve with buttered toast, an omelette and hot, black coffee. Is there anything more attractive than a man who cooks? Hint, hint.

Grilled Mushroom and Fresh Basil Salad

Portobello mushrooms 8, medium sized

Garlic 3–4 cloves, peeled and thinly sliced

Olive oil sufficient for drizzling

Salt to taste

Lime 1 large, squeezed for juice

Good-quality extra virgin olive oil 4 Tbsp

Shallots 2, peeled and finely minced

Salt 1 levelled tsp

Sugar ½ tsp

Freshly ground black pepper ¼ levelled tsp

Fresh basil leaves 2 handfuls, mixed, rinsed, drained

Plum tomatoes 2, ripe, firm, cut into wedges

- Wipe the mushrooms clean of any debris. Place them gill side up on the tray of a toaster oven, and scatter the gills with the sliced garlic.
- Drizzle evenly with olive oil and season with salt. Place tray in toaster oven and grill on high heat for 15 minutes.
- While waiting for mushrooms, combine the lime juice, extra virgin olive oil, chopped shallots, salt, sugar and pepper and whisk until salt and sugar dissolve. Set dressing aside.
- Arrange the mixed leaves and tomato wedges in a salad bowl or deep dish. When the mushrooms are done, remove from toaster and place on tomatoes and leaves in bowl.
- Drizzle all over with the dressing and serve immediately.

To Prepare: **15 minutes** To Cook: **15 minutes** Serves: **4**

light and yummy

INTERNATIONAL
Herald

This is perfect if you need to feed a small crowd but feel lazy–everything goes into one tray. Get large, firm tomatoes and small eggs so you don't have the eggs spilling over. Don't overcook the tomatoes or they will be tricky to lift off the rack. If you have cooked potatoes on hand, cut them up, put them under the bacon-wrapped sausages and let them crisp up as they absorb the smoky bacon drippings. This is so good, it's almost immoral. Forget "good intentions". The road to hell is really paved with bacon.

Languid Sunday Brunch

Large, firm tomatoes 4

Bacon 8 rashers

Coarse textured sausages 8, parboil for about 3 minutes if uncooked

Eggs 4

Melted butter 2–3 Tbsp

Salt to taste

Pepper to taste

- Set oven at 210°C. Cut a bit of the bottom off each tomato so that they can stand without rolling over. Slice off the tops of each tomato as well.
- Scoop out the centres from each tomato, taking care not to puncture the tomato shell. Discard or reserve for another use. Put tomatoes on a grilling rack fitted inside a baking tray.
- Wind a rasher of bacon around and down the length of each sausage. Place on rack, beside tomatoes. Break an egg into each tomato.
- Drizzle melted butter evenly over everything and season the eggs and tomatoes with salt. Sprinkle pepper over everything.
- Put tray in oven for about 12–15 minutes, or until eggs are cooked to your liking and bacon is crisp.
- Serve with lots of crusty buttered toast or fried potatoes, fresh fruit and black coffee.

To Prepare: **15 minutes** To Cook: **15 minutes** Serves: **4**

This is based on the Mexican quesadilla, a stuffed tortilla sandwich containing cheese, that's flattened and toasted, then cut into wedges and eaten as a snack or light meal. I'd run out of tortillas though, and only had naan in the freezer, hence the name. This is a breakfast version, but I think roast beef slices with cheddar and sliced radishes would be nice for lunch, or prawns with mango, mozzarella, chilli and coriander, if you're feeling adventurous.

Naanadilla Mexicana

Frozen naan 1,about 20-cm across, lightly toasted until thawed but not crisp

Small avocado ½, peeled and sliced

Ham 2 slices, cut into broad ribbons

Parmesan or Mozzarella cheese 6 small slices

Onion ½, peeled and sliced

Black olives 8, pitted and sliced

Green chilli 1, sliced, remove seeds if a milder level of spice is desired

Sour cream 2 Tbsp

Tomato ½, discard seeds and dice finely

- Layer all the ingredients except the sour cream and tomato on half of the naan. Fold empty half over the ingredients like you would a turnover.
- Slide onto the tray of a toaster oven and toast for 10–15 minutes or until naan is crusty and cheese is melted and oozing out from naan.
- Remove from toaster and press down firmly with your palm. Cut into 4 wedges and top with sour cream and diced tomato. Eat and enjoy.

Naan

To Prepare: **10 minutes** To Bake: **15 minutes** Serves: **2**

compares to you...

Sticky, chewy heaven

This is very loosely based on German *kuchen*, or cake, which is usually eaten at midmorning with coffee. That's why it's called a coffeecake, although it contains no coffee. It takes 5 minutes to get everything into and out of the mixing bowl, and 25 minutes from start to eating. The combination of cinnamon, butter, nuts and chocolate with lashings of maple syrup is almost orgasmic. Serve this at your next brunch gathering, if you dare.

Sticky Chocolate Nut Coffeecake

- Preheat oven at 190°C and grease a 20-cm square cake tin.
- Thoroughly combine the flour, baking soda and cream of tartar in a large bowl. Add sugar, yeast and cake spice or ground cinnamon. Thoroughly whisk the dry mixture until well mixed.
- Add to the dry mixture egg, buttermilk or yoghurt, water and vanilla. Stir with whisk until sugar and yeast are completely dissolved and there are no lumps.
- Pour batter into baking tin and evenly scatter the nuts and chocolate chips over batter. Bake for 15 minutes.
- Open oven door and evenly pour melted butter over cake. Take maple syrup bottle and drizzle a small amount evenly over cake. Don't overdo it or the top of the cake will scorch. Bake for another 5 minutes.
- Remove cake from oven and leave to cool for 10 minutes to allow topping to thicken. Cut into 8 or 12 pieces and serve as is, or with a blob of butter and drizzle of syrup.

Plain (all-purpose) flour 1¼ cups

Baking soda ½ levelled tsp

Cream of tartar 1 levelled tsp

Sugar ¼ cup

Instant yeast granules 1 tsp

Ground cake spice or ground cinnamon ½ levelled tsp

Egg 1

Buttermilk or plain yoghurt ¼ cup

Water ⅓ cup

Vanilla extract 1 tsp

Coarsely chopped almonds or pecans ½ cup or to taste

Dark chocolate chips ½ cup or to taste

Melted butter ¼ cup

Maple syrup squeeze bottle

To Prepare: **5 minutes** To Bake: **20 minutes** Serves: **4**

This is breakfast when you've only 5 minutes to spare. I use low-fat milk but full cream is fine if you prefer it. You can even add some cream if you're feeling indulgent. The oatmeal adds fibre and a lovely rich, malty flavour. This is low in fat and packed with calcium, protein and an army of vitamins and minerals. You'll wonder how something so healthy can taste so sinfully rich and creamy. You may never want anything else for breakfast again.

Berry Breakfast Whip

Very cold milk or plain, berry or vanilla-flavoured yoghurt 1 cup

Large, well-chilled strawberries 4, washed and hulled

Vanilla or berry-flavoured protein powder 2 rounded Tbsp

Uncooked oatmeal (optional) 2 slightly rounded Tbsp

Ice cubes 4 or 5 (if you like it really cold)

- Pop everything into a blender and blitz until very smooth and frothy.
- Pour into a tall glass and gulp down before running out the door. Now you're ready for anything that comes your way!

To Prepare: **5 minutes** Serves: **1 (or 2 small appetites)**

It's not the microwave that makes this "cheesy", it's the Parmesan. Scrambled eggs are one of the things that the microwave does better than a stove. They come out creamy as a dairy and lighter than a cloud. With microwave cooking though, you must be diligent with the stopping and stirring. Good results guaranteed, if you comply. It's that simple–no need to sign your soul over to the Devil. Just crack some eggs and open the microwave door. That's it–go on, it won't bite...

Cheesy Microwave Scrambled Eggs

- Put butter into a microwave-safe, roomy bowl and melt on High for 30 seconds. Remove bowl from microwave and break in all the eggs.
- Add salt and whisk thoroughly. Cook on High for 30 seconds, then remove from oven and stir with a fork.
- Return to oven and cook another 30 seconds on High. Remove bowl and stir with fork again, breaking up the bits of cooked egg.
- Return to oven and cook on High for 30 seconds. Remove and whisk with fork, breaking up eggs until they are creamy. Add cheese and stir.
- Return to oven and cook for a final 30 seconds on High. Remove and whisk thoroughly until creamy. Add pepper to taste and serve immediately.

Butter 2 generous Tbsp

Large eggs 4

Salt a fat pinch

Grated Parmesan cheese ½ cup or as much as you like

Pepper to taste

To Prepare: **5 minutes** To Cook: **3 minutes** Serves: **2**

It's the point of time in the day many of us look forward to. During the weekdays, it's a time where we can take a breather from work. During the weekends, it's a time to indulge in preparing something special for the family or for a gathering of friends. Whatever the reason, there is no better time or excuse one needs to whip up meals that are, needless to say, quick, easy and dizzily delicious to the very last drop and forkful.

Noon

This makes a great light lunch or vegetarian meal, and is wonderful with steak or roast chicken. You could substitute the feta cheese with *paneer* (fresh Indian curd cheese) or even bean curd. When buying avocados, look for evenly ripe ones without any soft or hard spots or dark brown spots on the skin.

Avocado, Green Chilli and Feta Salad

Small ripe avocados 2, cut into large cubes

Firm ripe tomatoes 2, cut as for avocados

Small red onion 1, sliced thickly

Green chillies 2–3, seeded and thickly sliced

Feta cheese 150 g, cut into cubes

Sesame seeds 2 tsp, toasted

Dressing

Lime juice 2 Tbsp

Extra virgin olive oil 2 Tbsp

Salt to taste

Chilli flakes (optional) ½ tsp

Freshly ground black pepper to taste

Note: To cube avocado, run knife vertically around the avocado from stem end to bottom and back again, all the way through to the stone. Grasp the cut halves of the avocado and twist each half in opposite directions. You will feel the stone dislodge. One half of the avocado will still have the stone in it. Holding the avocado halve with the stone firmly in hand, hit the stone sharply with the cutting edge of the knife, which will embed itself in the stone. Twist the knife sharply and quickly. The stone will come off and remain on the knife blade. Discard stone, peel avocado halves and cut into cubes.

- Combine avocados, tomatoes, onion, chilli and feta in a large bowl.
- Mix dressing ingredients and stir until salt dissolves.
- Pour dressing over salad ingredients and toss gently.
- Serve sprinkled with sesame seeds.

To Prepare: **10 minutes** Serves: **4**

Caldo verde means "green soup" and is Portugal's great equalizer; it cuts through social and economic boundaries and is loved by all in its country of origin. I won't make any claims on authenticity but this stuff is seriously, sinfully, delicious. If you have it, adding Portuguese white Vinho Verde (young or "green" wine) to the pot might make it more authentic. A glass of it, well-chilled, would go very nicely with the finished soup too. Serve with chunks of crusty baguette for a light but satisfying meal.

Caldo Verde

- Heat oil over high heat in a deep-frying pan or pot and brown sausage. Remove from pan, reserving oil. Set sausage aside.
- Add onion and garlic to pan and brown gently. Add chilli flakes and grated potatoes and stir for a few minutes. Add vermouth or Vinho Verde and stir for about 2 minutes.
- Add chicken stock and garlic powder, stir and bring to the boil. Lower heat and simmer, covered, for about 15 minutes.
- Ladle two-thirds of soup into a heatproof blender and blend into a purée. Pour puréed soup back into pan and return to the boil. Add sausage and kale or cabbage, stir and simmer gently for no more than 5 minutes. Make sure the kale is still green.
- Season to taste and serve immediately.

Olive oil 4 Tbsp

Spicy garlic coarse textured sausage 200 g, halved lengthwise, thickly sliced

Onion 1, medium, chopped

Garlic 4 cloves, minced

Chilli flakes 1 levelled tsp

Yukon Gold, or any other variety of creamy or waxy potatoes 3, peeled and coarsely grated

White vermouth or Vinho Verde 1 cup

Chicken stock (see page 158) 6 cups

Garlic powder 1½ levelled tsp

Kale or dark green cabbage 200 g, washed well, drained and shredded

Salt 1 levelled tsp or to taste

Sugar a pinch

Note: If using a stick, immersion or handheld blender, place blade in the centre of the pot of soup and blend in a circular motion, until the soup is as smooth or chunky as you like. To avoid splashes and scalds, make sure the blender blade is completely immersed and touching the bottom of the pot before you turn it on. Please use with caution, especially around children, and never let a child handle any kind of blender without adult supervision.

To Prepare: **15 minutes** To Cook: **25 minutes** Serves: **4**

Bocconcini are little balls of fresh mozzarella packed in brine. They are a world away from what often passes as "mozzarella"–gooey, stringy cheese that typically suffocates pizza. Traditionally made from buffalo milk, it has a lovely, soft, chewy, almost velvety texture and a mild, creamy flavour. The richness of the olive oil, the heat of the chilli and the mellow acidity of balsamic vinegar provide a stunning contrast to the mozzarella. This makes a beautiful appetiser that is child's play to put together.

Bocconcini with Basil, Balsamico and Chilli

Bocconcini balls 8, well-drained

Salt ¼ tsp , or to taste

Fresh large basil leaves 12–16, rinsed and drained

Extra virgin olive oil 2 Tbsp

Balsamic vinegar (*balsamico*) 1 Tbsp

Bird's eye chillies 2, seeded and very thinly sliced

Freshly ground black pepper to taste

- Gently pull apart each bocconcini until it resembles an open flower and place four on each of two plates. Sprinkle a little salt evenly over each bocconcini.
- Casually tear the basil and scatter half over each plate.
- Drizzle first the olive oil, then the balsamic vinegar evenly over each plate and scatter the sliced chillies over.
- Give each plate a good grinding of black pepper and serve immediately.

To Prepare: **10 minutes** Serves: **2**

Even if you're resolutely carnivorous, these peppers, or capsicums will make a believer out of you. They taste like wood-fired oven pizzas, only better. Sweet, smoky, earthy, savoury and very, satisfying. They make a gorgeous light starter for 4, or vegetarian main course for 2, served with buttered noodles and a light green salad. To me, they taste their best grabbed off the plate and bitten greedily into. Watch out for the steaming juices. A glass of Pinot Noir or Dolcetto would make an excellent "chaser".

Baked Feta Stuffed Peppers

- Preheat oven at 220°C.
- Combine diced bread, feta cheese, garlic, salt, pepper, oregano and paprika in a large bowl. Divide stuffing amongst the pepper halves, patting lightly into place.
- Drizzle peppers and stuffing evenly with olive oil and put peppers into oven. Bake for 10 minutes, then reduce temperature to 180°C and continue to bake for 5 minutes. Peppers should be tender, and stuffing golden and crusty by this time.
- Remove from oven and serve immediately.

Bread 1 slice, diced

Feta cheese 80 g, diced

Garlic 2 cloves, finely chopped

Salt ¼ tsp

Pepper ½ tsp

Dried oregano ½ tsp

Paprika powder ½ tsp

Bell peppers (capsicums) 2, halved, remove seeds and core but leave stems intact

Olive oil sufficient for drizzling

To Prepare: **15 minutes** To Bake: **15 minutes** Serves: **2–4**

When cooking squid, do so no more than 3 minutes, or no less than 30 minutes. Anything in between and you will have rubber, albeit tasty rubber. This is one of those 3-minute instances. Keep the heat high and have the squid in and out of the pan quickly. This is just beautiful to look at and the combination of crusty seared squid, luscious buttery avocado and fiery harissa borders on the orgasmic. Eat it and see if you disagree. Serve as is or with savoury rice (see page 100) or onion cous cous (see page 72).

Pan-seared Squid with Avocado and Harissa

Squid 500 g, cleaned and cut at an angle into thin, broad slices

Ripe avocados 2, cut flesh into large dice (see page 38 on avocado preparation method)

Salt to taste

Extra virgin olive oil to taste

Freshly crushed black pepper to taste

Harissa

Fresh red chillies 3, sliced thickly

Hot red chilli flakes 2 tsp

Fresh coriander (cilantro) leaves 1 handful

Garlic 3 cloves

Cumin seeds ½ tsp, ground

Extra virgin olive oil 1½ Tbsp

Lemon juice 1½ Tbsp

Salt 1 levelled tsp or to taste

Sugar ½ levelled tsp

- Prepare harissa. Combine ingredients in a blender and process to a slightly chunky consistency. Set aside.
- Heat about 1 Tbsp oil in a pan over high heat until smoking. Very quickly cook the squid pieces on both sides until lightly charred for no more than 3 minutes. Keep the heat high and don't overcook. Don't overcrowd the pan or the squid's natural juices will start to leak out as the temperature of the pan drops and loses its ability to seal off the surface of the squid. Remove from pan and set squid aside.
- Gently combine avocado with the harissa in a large bowl. Taste and add more salt if necessary.
- Divide the avocado into 2 equal portions between two plates. Divide the squid between the two plates, laying it over the avocado. Drizzle lightly with extra virgin olive oil. Sprinkle salt and pepper over the squid. Serve immediately.

tasty rubber? not! melti

To Prepare: **25 minutes** To Cook: **5 minutes** Serves: **2**

gly tender squid? Yes!

It's nothing more than crumbed and fried eggplant, but I love crunching through the crusty top and tearing into the tender, moist core. This is fantastic as a nibble with drinks, in the Spanish *tapas* tradition. The seasoning is shockingly simple but this is a perfect example of how something really can add up to more than the sum of its parts. Try this with grilled steak or fish. Also very good with mild curried lamb, chicken or fish and rice.

Salt and Pepper Eggplant

Long purple eggplant (aubergine/brinjal) 2, each about 30-cm long

Salt 1 levelled tsp

Sugar (optional) ½ levelled tsp

White pepper 1 levelled tsp

Uncooked rice 2 Tbsp, finely ground

Plain (all-purpose) flour 1 Tbsp

- Cut tops off eggplants. Halve lengthwise and cut each half across into 4 segments. You will end up with 16 pieces, each about 7½ cm long. Score the cut surfaces of the eggplant.
- Combine salt, sugar and pepper thoroughly in a small bowl.Season all the cut surfaces of the eggplant pieces. Heat about 1 cup of oil in a deep pan. I find that a round bottom Chinese wok works best for deep frying without too much oil.
- Combine ground rice and plain flour on a plate. Coat the cut surfaces of the eggplant with the flour and rice mixture. Fry the eggplant briefly in the hot oil, turning often, until crisp and golden. Take care not to burn the skin or it will be bitter.
- Drain on paper towels and serve with a squeeze of lime if you like.

To Prepare: **7 minutes** To Cook: **10 minutes** Serves: **4**

I eat these by the plateful when I'm depressed. Better than ice cream, trust me. My favourite way to serve this is to make lots to go with drinks, along with the Salt and Pepper Eggplant (see page 48). Just put them in little dishes and provide lots of toothpicks so guests can pick and "graze" at leisure. I peel the potatoes but you can leave the skins on if you prefer.

Chilli Garlic Potatoes

Cooking oil or vegetable oil 3 Tbsp

Fresh red chillies 4, pound to a paste

Garlic 5 cloves, peeled and finely chopped

New potatoes 250 g, peeled, washed then drained

Water 2 cups

Salt 1 levelled tsp or to taste

Sugar (optional) ½ levelled tsp

- Heat oil in a deep pan over medium heat. When hot, add pounded chillies and fry for about 3–5 minutes.
- Add garlic and continue to fry until fragrant and the mixture begins to crisp up and exude oil.
- Add potatoes and stir for about 2 minutes to coat potatoes with the chilli mixture. Pour in 2 cups water and bring to the boil. Add salt and sugar and stir.
- Lower heat and cover. Simmer, stir and turn potatoes occasionally to ensure even cooking, until water evaporates and potatoes are thickly coated with chilli paste. By then, they should be tender right through but with their shape retained.
- Dish out and serve.

To Prepare: **10 minutes** To Cook: **20 minutes** Serves: **4**

This is bursting with flavour and loaded with antioxidants and natural antibiotics. Nothing knocks a head cold off its feet better or faster than this, and nothing goes better with a nurse's uniform. You think "Jewish Penicillin" is something? You ain't seen nothing yet. One whiff and two bowls of this will have you back on your feet (and playing doctor again) in no time.

Florence Nightingale Soup

Garlic 4 cloves, peeled

Fresh ginger 5-cm length, scraped

White peppercorns 1 tsp, crushed

Chicken ½, plump, halved and skin left intact

Hot pepper or chilli flakes ½ tsp or to taste

Turmeric powder 1 levelled tsp

Tomato 1, large, cut into 8

Lemon grass 4 stalks, top half discarded and ends bruised

Kaffir lime leaves 8

Salt 1 tsp or to taste

Granulated chicken stock 2 tsp or to taste

Light soy sauce 2 Tbsp

Fresh coriander (cilantro) leaves ½ cup, torn

- Pound or blend the garlic, ginger and crushed white peppercorns to a smooth paste, using a little water.
- Combine everything except coriander leaves in a pot and pour in enough water to cover the chicken. Bring to the boil, then lower heat, cover pot and simmer for about 30 minutes or until thigh meat is no longer pink at the bone. Reduce heat to minimum and keep soup hot.
- Remove chicken from stock and cool until comfortable enough to handle. Tear off meat from chicken in long strips and put into individual soup bowls. Top up with hot stock.
- Garnish with coriander and serve immediately.

To Prepare: **10 minutes** To Cook: **30 minutes** Serves: **4**

Live cockles will open their shells when left alone. Ensure the ones you buy are alive and well. Scrub shells and wash thoroughly. All three featured dips are searingly hot and perfectly complement the very distinct flavour of cockles. This dish is an acquired taste but once hooked, you will find yourself in the grip of a lifelong addiction. These and cold, cold beer are a heaven-appointed match. Eat as is, with white rice or hot crusty fries–if you're adventurous enough for a transcontinental culinary leap.

Cockles with Three Dips

- Combine ginger, crushed peppercorns, salt, sugar, vinegar and water in a blender and blend into a very smooth paste.
- Remove a third of the sauce from blender and set aside.
- To make the wasabi dip, remove half the remaining sauce from blender and stir in the wasabi. Set aside.
- Add chilli and garlic to the remaining sauce in the blender and blend until smooth. Set aside.
- Bring a wide and relatively shallow pot of water to boil. This will allow cockles to boil in one even layer so all will be uniformly cooked. When water boils, add washed and drained cockles. Allow to boil madly for 30 seconds.
- Turn off heat and drain cockles immediately. Discard any cockles that have not opened after cooking. Serve immediately with the dips and steaming hot white rice if you wish.

Fresh ginger 75 g, peeled

White peppercorns 2 tsp, crushed

Salt 1½ levelled tsp or to taste

Sugar ½ levelled tsp or to taste

White vinegar 1½Tbsp

Boiled water ⅓ cup

Prepared wasabi paste 1 tsp

Bird's eye chillies 4

Garlic 2 cloves, large, peeled

Live cockles 1 kg, thoroughly washed, soaked for 5 minutes and drained

To Prepare: **20 minutes** To Cook: **30 seconds** Serves: **2–3**

Don't Be afraid
To make a mess!

Roll up your sleeves, prepare to get down and dirty and forget everything they taught you at finishing school. You'll be sweating and cursing, biting and sucking, nibbling and drooling, sweet, sticky juices will be flowing ... and I can almost guarantee, you'll be loving every minute, unless, you don't like fresh crab, bathed in a chilli and ginger-spiked shrimp relish sauce, bursting with the sweet and salty tang of the sea. Serve with copious amounts of white rice and frigidly cold beer. Oh, and don't wear anything white.

Crabs with Hot Ginger and Shrimp Sauce

Large live Sri Lankan crabs 4, about 600 g each, cleaned, chop each crab across into half and crack the claws

White wine, sherry or vermouth ⅓ cup

Fresh ginger 5-cm length, peeled and finely shredded

Garlic 6 cloves, minced

Fermented shrimp relish (*cincalok*) 2 levelled Tbsp

Bird's eye chillies 6, chopped

Salt (optional) ½ tsp

Freshly squeezed lime juice 1 Tbsp

- Put crabs in a large non-reactive bowl and pour over the wine, sherry or vermouth. Mix thoroughly and set aside.
- Fill bottom of a steamer with water and bring to the boil. When water boils, remove crabs from the bowl, leaving behind the wine or sherry and place crabs on a plate. Reserve wine and set aside. Steam crabs on maximum heat for 8–10 minutes. Check the crab for doneness. Don't overcook.
- 5 minutes into steaming crab, heat a wok and add about 2 Tbsp oil. When smoking hot, add the ginger, garlic and shrimp relish. Stir over high heat until fragrant and almost crisp.
- Add chillies and the reserved wine. Stir, simmer and taste. Add salt if necessary. Crabs should be done by now. Remove from steamer and gently pour crabs and cooking juices into wok. Stir until combined. Add lime juice and stir again. Turn off heat.
- Dish out and serve with extra lime wedges if you like.

Note : To kill crabs, without untying their restraints, turn them onto their backs. Lift up the triangular flap and drive the point of a sharp knife all the way down into the cleft under the triangular flap. The crab will die instantly and without much pain. If "crabicide" turns your stomach, ask the fishmonger to do it for you, if you're sure you are going to cook the crab as soon as you get home. Crabs should not be killed except immediately prior to cooking as once dead, they deteriorate rapidly.

Shrimp relish or *cincalok* is made from salted and fermented krill. In parts of Southeast Asia it is usually livened up with fresh chilli, raw onion and lime juice and eaten with fried fish and rice. If you can't get fermented shrimp relish, substitute with 1 Tbsp Thai fish sauce and 1 Tbsp finely minced onion.

To Prepare: 20 minutes **To Cook:** 10–12 minutes **Serves:** 4

This looks to me like vegetable confetti strewn on pasta. The garlic and anchovies are a feature of this dish and somehow echo the robust, sun-drenched flavours of that well known Mediterranean classic, ratatouille. Be careful with the salt as you won't need much because of the anchovies and capers. Have you seen anything prettier or sunnier on a plate?

Confetti Spaghetti

Dried spaghetti 250 g

Olive oil 4 Tbsp

Garlic 8 cloves, peeled and chopped

Anchovy fillets 8, drained

Chilli flakes ½ tsp

Purple eggplant (aubergine/brinjal) 2 cups, diced

Firm red tomatoes 1 cup, diced

Yellow cherry tomatoes 1 cup, quartered

Capers 2 levelled Tbsp, rinsed

Parsley or coriander (cilantro) leaves ½ cup, chopped

Salt to taste

Pepper to taste

- Prepare pasta according to package instructions. Your pasta should already be boiling for about 2 minutes in the pot when you start your pasta sauce. This way, your pasta and sauce will both be done at the same time.
- Heat olive oil in a large pan over medium heat. Add garlic, anchovies and chilli flakes and brown gently, stirring all the time. When fragrant, add eggplant and cook gently until tender but not mushy.
- Add red and yellow tomatoes and stir to mix. Cook for about 1 minute, then add capers. By this time, your spaghetti should be done.Remove from pot, drain and add to the pan along with about ⅓ cup of the boiling liquid.
- Combine gently and season if necessary.
- Transfer to a platter or individual dishes and garnish with coriander or parsley and a drizzle of extra virgin olive oil. Serve immediately.

To Prepare: 15 minutes **To Cook:** 10 minutes **Serves:** 4

azy with colour!

I know these veer dangerously close to trashy but man does not live on posh nosh alone. A little kitsch is good for the soul and these are just what the soul doctor prescribed. Who cares if they're not glamorous or trendy when these salmon rice cakes taste so wantonly good? They're wonderfully crunchy outside, creamy inside and are guaranteed to return the soul to perfect equilibrium. Dip in ketchup and wash down with hot tea or coffee. Eat at least once a month; soul doctor's orders.

Fried Salmon Rice Cakes

Cold cooked rice 3 cups

Salt ½ levelled tsp or to taste

Garlic powder 1½ tsp

Pepper ½ levelled tsp

Canned salmon in brine 1 can, about 185 g, drained

Chopped spring onions (scallions), parsley or coriander (cilantro) leaves 2 Tbsp

Egg 1, beaten

Soft breadcrumbs 1 cup

- Combine rice, salt, garlic powder and pepper in a large mixing bowl and mash thoroughly using your hand. Add salmon and mash into the rice until smooth. Add chopped spring onion, parsley or coriander leaves and mix in lightly but thoroughly.
- Form mixture into thick patties and dip in beaten egg. Roll in breadcrumbs, pressing them on and dusting off excess. Fry in moderately hot oil until golden and crusty.
- Drain on crushed paper towels. Serve immediately with a sharp chunky tomato sauce and green salad for a light and easy lunch. I actually eat this dipped in wasabi, and drink green tea after. Not strange at all. Try it.

To Prepare: **15 minutes** To Cook: **10 minutes** Serves: **4**

This takes barely 20 minutes to put together, from the time you light the stove to the moment everyone sits down and tucks in. If you can get pancetta (Italian bacon) so much the better but if not, regular bacon will serve well enough. Try to get really ripe Roma tomatoes as they have more flavour. The aroma of smoky bacon and garlic frying may be enough to get your neighbours inviting themselves over for lunch.

Pasta with Bacon, Tomatoes and Garlic

Garlic 8 cloves, peeled and finely chopped

Bacon 200 g, cut into large dice

Firm ripe tomatoes 3, medium, cut into large dice

Short pasta like penne, farfalle or fusilli 300 g

Salt 1½ levelled tsp

Freshly crushed black pepper ½ levelled tsp

Garlic powder 1 levelled tsp

Coriander (cilantro) leaves ½ cup, coarsely chopped

- Cook pasta in boiling water for about 10 minutes. When pasta has been boiling for about 6 minutes, heat 3 Tbsp olive oil in a pan over medium heat and gently fry garlic. After a minute, add bacon and stir for about 3 minutes.
- Add tomatoes and increase heat. By this time, pasta should be ready. Remove from pot, drain and add to pan. Stir everything to combine. Add salt, pepper and garlic powder. Stir until thoroughly combined and add coriander leaves. Stir again, then turn off heat.
- Transfer to a platter or individual dishes and serve immediately.

To Prepare: **6 minutes** To Cook: **12 minutes** Serves: **4**

Bang! this baby

Alright, it's not that hot but the list of ingredients does give the impression that this will leave heat blisters on the insides of your mouth. Not so. It's more piquant than out-and-out hot and also incredibly smoky, savoury and lick-the-plate-clean delicious. Serve this with white rice, tossed through cooked fine spaghetti or blanched Chinese egg noodles. You could cook it all in one pan, instead of frying the bacon, ginger, onion and chilli separately but I have to warn you, the texture and appearance will suffer a little.

Gun Smoke Chicken

Deboned whole chicken legs 600 g, skinned, cut into bite-size chunks and drained well

White vinegar 1½ Tbsp

Prepared wasabi paste 2 levelled tsp

Ground black pepper 1 levelled tsp

Back or streaky bacon 6 rashers, sliced into thick strips

Red onion 1, medium, peeled and sliced

Fresh red chillies 3, sliced

Fresh ginger 5-cm length, peeled and finely shredded

Salt ½ levelled tsp or to taste

- Combine chicken, vinegar, wasabi and pepper in a large bowl. Mix thoroughly and set aside.
- Heat about 2 Tbsp oil in a wok until smoking. Fry chicken on high heat, for about 10 minutes, stirring often.
- While chicken cooks, heat 1 Tbsp oil in a separate pan until smoking and fry bacon on high heat until beginning to crisp and oil seeps out.
- If chicken starts to scorch in other pan, lower heat.
- Add onion, chillies and ginger to bacon and stir on high heat until fragrant and ginger and bacon are brown and crisp at edges. Add this mixture to the chicken in the other pan. Stir, taste and add salt if necessary. Stir to combine.
- Dish out and serve immediately.

shot me down...

To Prepare: **15 minutes** To Cook: **10 minutes** Serves: **2–4**

This might be my favourite pasta dish, if I had to choose one. It's visually stunning and always tempts me into eating, even if I'm not particularly hungry. That's what I call seduction. I haven't even begun to tell you how the smell of the bacon, shallots and vermouth sizzling in the pan will almost certainly quicken your pulse. What more can I say? Cook, eat!

Pasta with Bacon, Broad Beans and Vermouth

Frozen broad beans 300 g

Shell pasta, linguine or spaghetti 250–300 g

Olive oil 3 Tbsp

Bacon 200 g, diced

Shallots 4, chopped

Garlic 4 cloves, chopped

White vermouth (Martini Bianco) or Pernod ½ glass

Salt to taste

Pepper to taste

- Fill a deep pot half-full with water and boil.
- Put frozen beans into a covered bowl and microwave on High for 2 minutes. Peel off skins and set aside.
- Cook pasta according to package instructions. When pasta has been boiling for about 3 minutes, heat a pan on medium heat and add olive oil, followed by diced bacon.
- When bacon starts to splutter and crisp, add shallots, garlic and broad beans and cook for about 3 minutes, then add vermouth. Boil down until concentrated.
- By this time, pasta should be ready. Remove from pot, drain and add to pan. Spoon in a few tablespoons of the pasta cooking water and stir everything. Add seasoning to taste. Mix well and turn off heat.
- Divide pasta amongst four plates. Drizzle with extra virgin olive oil and grate over some parmesan if you like. I like to garnish long pasta with chopped parsley or coriander. Serve immediately.

To Prepare: 20 minutes **To Cook:** 10 minutes **Serves:** 4

Eat me! Mi So yummy!

Look for loosely grained flesh when buying beef. A tight grain and flesh that springs back firmly when pressed means tough meat. This is lovely with white rice or over blanched broad rice noodles. If you're having this with noodles, increase the water to ½ cup and the oyster sauce to 4 Tbsp. Spoon the beef and gravy over the noodles and garnish with scallions, crisp fried shallots and sesame oil. Hits the spot, every time.

Sliced Beef with Miso and Chilli

- Combine beef slices and flour and mix well. Heat 2 Tbsp oil in a wok and when really hot, fry beef until it changes colour. Remove from pan and set aside.
- Add 1 Tbsp oil to the same wok and when hot, fry garlic, miso paste and chilli flakes over medium heat until fragrant. Add oyster sauce, stir for a minute, then add sugar and water. Stir and bring to the boil.
- Add mushrooms and return beef to the wok. Stir briefly, then taste and adjust seasoning if necessary.
- Turn off heat, dish out and garnish with spring onions. Serve immediately.

Rump steak 400 g, sliced thinly across the grain

Plain (all-purpose) flour 2 tsp

Garlic 4 cloves, minced

Miso paste 2 tsp

Chilli flakes 1 tsp

Oyster sauce 2 Tbsp

Fresh shiitake, cremini or Swiss brown mushrooms a handful, thickly sliced

Sugar ½ tsp

Water ¼ cup

Spring onions (scallions) preferred amount, cut into 5-cm lengths

To Prepare: **5 minutes** To Cook: **8 minutes** Serves: **2–3**

This is my lazy day mac and cheese–no need to stir up your *roux* from scratch and I actually think the canned soup makes it far tastier. The sour cream lifts it out of the ordinary and the garlic gives it enough edge to kick it soundly out of the "nursery food" category. Yes, this is mac and cheese, all grown up, with bite and attitude. This goes marvellously with a glass of chilled Chardonnay or Pinot Gris. Who says you can't slum in style?

Chicken Soup Mac and Cheese

Elbow macaroni, fusilli or shell pasta 350 g

Campbell's condensed cream of chicken soup 2 cans

Water 1½ cups

Sharp Cheddar or Gouda cheese 1 cup, grated

Garlic powder 1 levelled tsp

Ground white pepper ½ levelled tsp

Salt ½ levelled tsp

Sour cream ½ cup

Parmesan cheese 1 cup, grated

Breadcrumbs ½ cup

Garlic 2 cloves, peeled and finely chopped

- Preheat oven to 230°C.
- Cook the macaroni or pasta in boiling water for about 8 minutes. It should be slightly undercooked as you will bake it for a further 15 minutes or so.
- While macaroni or pasta is cooking, put the condensed soup into a pot and add water. Stir briskly with a whisk and bring to the boil. Reduce heat and add in Cheddar or cheese of your choice. Whisk until cheese melts. Season with garlic powder, pepper and salt. You may not need the salt as there is plenty of sodium in the cheese but I like to add just a little. Taste sauce, adjust seasoning if necessary and turn off heat.
- The macaroni should be done by now. Drain and put into pot of sauce. Stir well, then add sour cream and stir lightly. Taste and if to your liking, pour into a 20-cm by 30-cm baking dish. Don't leave any sauce behind in the pot; scrape it all off into the baking dish.
- Combine the Parmesan, bread crumbs and garlic and scatter evenly over the macaroni. Put into oven and bake for 10–15 minutes or until topping is crusty.
- Remove from oven and cool at least 5 minutes before cutting and serving.

To Prepare: 5 minutes **To Cook:** 25 minutes **Serves:** 4 (1 if depressed)

me comfort food!

This is a Sephardic Jewish dish and *shakshouka* is Hebrew for shaky or wobbly, probably a reference to how the eggs should be. This is comfort food supreme. The contrasting flavours and textures of the crusty potatoes, the chewy, robustly seasoned beef and the soothingly tender, creamy eggs make this a joy to eat.

Shakshouka

- Preheat oven to 200°C.
- Heat oil in a deep pan or frying pan. Brown onion and garlic and when fragrant and transparent, add eggplant.
- Stir for about 2–3 minutes, then add beef. Turn up heat and stir, breaking up beef until it changes colour.
- Add chilli flakes, garlic powder, tomato paste, salt, pepper and sugar. Stir until well-mixed and colour has deepened. Add water or chicken stock, stir and simmer until slightly thick. Taste and adjust seasoning if necessary.
- Transfer meat and tomato mixture to a 20-cm by 30-cm baking dish. Spread out evenly and make 4 depressions in the mixture with a soup ladle or small cup. Break an egg into each depression and drizzle a little oil over each egg.
- Bake uncovered for 10 minutes for slightly runny eggs and 15 minutes for firm eggs. Serve sprinkled with parsley or coriander and fried potatoes on the side.

Olive or vegetable oil 4 Tbsp

Large onion 1, peeled and chopped

Garlic 6 cloves, peeled and chopped

Eggplant (aubergine/brinjal) ½, medium, diced

Minced beef 300 g

Chilli flakes 1 levelled tsp

Garlic powder ½ levelled tsp

Tomato paste 4 Tbsp

Salt 1 levelled tsp or to taste

Pepper ½ tsp

Sugar ¼ tsp

Water or chicken stock (see page 158) 2½ cups

Eggs 4

To Prepare: **10 minutes** To Cook: **20 minutes** Serves: **4**

Dinner; the time and the meal that we devote the most amount of attention to, because it's the end of the day and the beginning of untold possibilties. Whether you're in the mood for a little romance, seeking the camaraderie of good friends, the warmth of family or simply in need of a little soul-soothing balm to ease the strain of a hard day, you'll find something here that answers the call. The recipes in this chapter are hardly time consuming, but give gratifying results. Recommended trimmings: music to cook to, a lively imagination, sparkling conversation, and *voila*! Dinner is served. The rest is up to you...

Night

This is a wonderfully simple yet evocative meal that brings to mind a feast in a secluded, jasmine-scented, candle lit courtyard in Morocco. Harissa sauce (page 46) would perfectly complement the rich, smoky lamb and succulent cous cous. The salad component is a mix of seeded and coarsely chopped cucumber, fresh coriander and red and green chillies, bound with a little yoghurt, seasoned with salt and a squeeze of lime. Oops! Forgot the nubile dancing maidens and handsome wine steward! Damn.

Cumin and Pepper Lamb Chops with Onion Cous Cous

Black peppercorns 1½ tsp

Cumin seeds 1½ tsp

Salt 2 levelled tsp

Lamb loin chops 8, leave the fat on

Water or chicken stock (see page 158) 1 cup

Olive oil 2 Tbsp

Instant cous cous 1cup

Red onions 2, medium, peeled and sliced into thick rings

- Combine pepper, cumin and 1 tsp salt and pound to a coarse powder. Wipe the lamb chops dry with paper towels and season well with the pounded salt and spice mixture. Set aside.
- Heat the water or stock, remaining salt and 1 Tbsp olive oil in a pot and when boiling, turn off heat. Stir in the couscous and when combined, cover and set aside for 3 minutes.
- Heat the remaining olive oil in a pan and sear the onions until lightly charred and fragrant. Fluff up cous cous and stir in onions lightly until evenly combined. Taste and adjust seasoning.
- Heat the same pan, without adding any oil, until smoking and cook the lamb chops for about 2 minutes each side. Do not overcook.
- Dish out cous cous and arrange lamb chops over or alongside cous cous. Serve with harissa sauce (see page 46) and a green salad if you like.

To Prepare: 20 minutes **To Cook:** 7 minutes **Serves:** 4

Be spellbound by a little moroccan magic...

Ginseng is widely believed to aid in overcoming physical trauma. I drink this often, to hasten recovery from sport injuries. It is also thought to be a very potent aid to, *um*, potency, as it speeds up sluggish circulations, both in men and women. This may sound purely medicinal but I think you will be surprised by how tasty it really is. Try adding blanched fine noodles and a drizzle of sesame oil to the strained hot liquid. This is hubby's favourite broth because after 2 bowls, "almost any woman looks beautiful". *Harrumph.*

Beef, Ginseng and Wolfberry Tea

Water 5 cups

Lean beef like chuck steaks 200 g

Small dried whole ginseng roots 2, rinsed

Small red apple 1, cored, quartered and seeds discarded

Wolfberries ¼ cup, rinsed

Salt (optional) 1 levelled tsp

Note : Ginseng may elevate blood pressure and should be avoided by those with related medical conditions. If on medication, check with your doctor regarding drug interactions before consuming ginseng.

- Combine all ingredients except salt in a pot. Cook from start to finish, on minimum heat, for 30 minutes.
- Make sure the liquid never goes beyond a gentle simmer throughout cooking time. Turn off heat and add salt if desired.
- After you've drunk all the liquid, add another 5 cups water and repeat the cooking process before discarding the ingredients. The resulting "tea" will not be as potent as the first time but will still have nutritional value and flavour.
- To aid recovery from physical injury, drink the liquid at night, before retiring for 5 consecutive nights. Wait 5 days and repeat if necessary.
- Drink the liquid 3 alternate nights a week for other "purposes". **Cough*.*

To Prepare: **5 minutes** To Cook: **30 minutes** Serves: **1–2**

This is very easy, takes only a 15-minute blast in the oven and is perfect when you need something impressive in a hurry. The beauty of the salsa is that it does double duty–as the "sauce" and the vegetable. Crusty roasted potatoes would complement this beautifully. If you're planning a Valentine's Dinner for your beloved, it may interest you to know that the French used to call tomatoes "love apples" and onions have long been considered an aphrodisiac. Muse, muse.

Pork Tenderloin with Warm Onion and Tomato Salsa

Garlic powder 1 levelled tsp

Chilli flakes ½ levelled tsp

Black pepper 1 levelled tsp

White pepper 1 levelled tsp

Sugar 1 levelled tsp

Salt 1 levelled tsp

Pork tenderloin 1, about 400 g

Olive oil 4 Tbsp

Salsa

Olive oil 2 Tbsp

Tomatoes 3, chopped up into rough chunks

Red onions 2, chopped up into chunks, smaller than tomato chunks

Garlic powder 1 tsp

Chilli flakes 1 tsp

Lemon juice 1 Tbsp

Salt 1 levelled tsp or to taste

Sugar ¼ tsp or to taste

Water or chicken stock (see page 158) ¾ cup

- Set oven at 250°C.
- Combine garlic, chilli, black and white pepper, sugar and salt and sprinkle evenly over tenderloin. Rub in well, then place in a large bowl and pour olive oil over. Rub oil in until fully absorbed. Set aside.
- Prepare salsa. Heat oil in a frying pan and when smoking hot, add tomatoes and onions. Stir for a few seconds. Keep heat high and work quickly to keep tomatoes and onions crunchy. Add in all other ingredients, stir, taste and adjust seasoning if necessary. Turn off heat and set aside.
- Heat a heavy-based pan and when smoking, put in tenderloin. Sear one side for about 30 seconds, then turn over and do the same for the other side. Keep the heat high. When done, transfer to a roasting rack set into a roasting tin.
- Roast in the oven for 10 minutes, then reduce heat to 170°C and roast for another 5 minutes. Remove from oven and leave to cool for 15 minutes before carving. Serve with salsa, and roasted potatoes or buttered noodles.

To Prepare: **15 minutes** To Cook: **18 minutes** Serves: **2–3**

"Calamari frito" means fried squid in Italian, and the simplicity of the name belies the fact that this is probably one of the most delicious things on earth that you could possibly put into your mouth. This is the most popular way of preparing and eating squid in Italy and it's a wisdom I can hardly argue with. Serve with chips and a fresh, lightly dressed green salad. Enough talking. Cook, then eat and sigh with pleasure.

Calamari Frito

- Thoroughly combine the cornmeal, flour, salt, pepper and paprika on a large plate. Slice squid tubes into thick rings. Halve the heads.
- Heat the oil in a deep pan over medium-high heat.
- While oil is heating, put squid pieces into the beaten egg and make sure they are thoroughly coated with egg. Lift half the squid out of the bowl and allow excess egg to drip off.
- Drop squid pieces lightly into flour mixture, ensuring they don't clump together. Toss them in the flour until evenly and thickly coated. Lightly shake off excess flour, then gently drop them individually into the hot oil. Fry until squid pieces turn crusty and golden. This should take barely 3 minutes.
- Remove squid pieces from oil and drain on paper towels. Repeat with the remaining squid.
- Squeeze lemon juice over. Eat immediately. Stop yourself from moaning, if you can.

Fine cornmeal ¼ cup

Plain (all-purpose) flour ¼ cup

Salt ½ levelled tsp

White pepper ½ levelled tsp

Paprika 1 levelled tsp

Squid 300 g, cleaned, skinned and well-drained

Vegetable oil 2 cups

Eggs 1, large, beaten in a large bowl

Lemon 1, small, cut into wedges

To Prepare: **20 minutes** To Cook: **6 minutes** Serves: **2**

This is inspired by those intriguing-looking relishes you get at Japanese and Korean restaurants, which initially seem pointless, until you start nibbling and find you can't stop and eventually need to ask for a second helping. It's a bit like kimchi and a bit like pickled daikon. The flavours are a maddeningly addictive mix of salty, sweet, hot, sour and savoury. If you like a riot of different flavours and textures tumbling about in your mouth, you will love this. This was made for white rice and grilled squid or octopus.

Daikon and Toasted Whitebait Salad

Tiny dried whitebait 3 Tbsp

Black sesame seeds 1 tsp

White sesame seeds 1 tsp

Daikon (white radish/mooli) 1, small, about 250 g, peeled, coarsely grated, squeezed dry of excess water

Chilli flakes 1 levelled tsp

Sugar 2 levelled tsp

Salt ¼–½ levelled tsp, adjust according to the saltiness of the whitebait

Fragrant sesame oil 2 tsp

Ponzu (Japanese citrus vinegar) 1 tsp

Spring onions (scallions) 1 thin stalk, shredded

- Heat a frying pan and dry-fry whitebait until almost crisp. Add black and white sesame seeds to the pan and continue toasting, stirring until fragrant and seeds begin to pop. Set aside.
- Combine grated and squeezed daikon, chilli flakes, sugar, salt, sesame oil and ponzu in a large bowl. Mix thoroughly.
- Tip in the toasted whitebait, sesame seeds and scallions. Toss lightly.
- Sprinkle with extra toasted sesame seeds if you like and serve.

To Prepare: **10 minutes** To Cook: **3–5 minutes** Serves: **2–3**

tably crunchy!

This is perfect for picking at with chopsticks and a glass of Shiraz when you're in the mood for a quiet evening at home with your beloved. It's also posh enough, though very easy to put together, to serve as a main course for two, or starter for four if you want to have a dinner party and show off just a little. For dinner, serve with blanched fine noodles dressed with light soy sauce and sesame oil. Believe me when I say this is so scrumptious, even those claiming not to like duck won't need much prompting.

Duck Breast with Warm Lime, Ginger and Plum Dressing

Duck breasts 2, skin left on, seasoned with salt and pepper rubbed in well

Fresh ginger 5-cm length, finely shredded

Large firm black plum 1, thinly sliced

Salt 1 levelled tsp

Sugar 2–3 levelled tsp

Pepper ½ levelled tsp

Lime juice 2 Tbsp, preferably from Thai green limes

Your favourite salad greens 70 g, washed thoroughly and drained well, or use baby spinach leaves

Extra shredded ginger (optional) sufficient to garnish

- Heat a heavy based pan until smoking, then lower duck breasts in with the skin side down. You won't need any oil as duck is very fatty.
- When the fat starts to seep out, lower heat to medium and continue cooking. After 4 minutes total, flip breasts over and cook other side for 4 minutes as well. Remove from pan and allow to cool.
- Add shredded ginger to hot duck fat in pan and stir briefly. Add plum and stir for barely half a minute. Add salt, sugar, pepper and lime juice. Stir well and taste. If to your satisfaction, turn off heat immediately and set aside.
- Mound salad greens or baby spinach on a platter. You may like to include red pepper or carrots strips for some colour. Slice duck breast across into thin slices and arrange attractively on platter beside salad.
- Drizzle the warm dressing over the duck and greens. Garnish with more shredded ginger if desired and serve immediately.

To Prepare: **20 minutes** To Cook: **9 minutes** Serves: **2–4**

This is inspired by both Bulgogi and Bibimbap, Korean restaurant staples. Use sirloin or rib eye if you're in an extravagant mood, brisket or rump if you're feeling frugal. Whichever you choose, slice the beef as thinly as you can and don't stint on the sesame oil. This is divine with kimchi and *soju*, a Korean rice wine that tastes mild but after 4 glasses, makes you wish you hadn't quite so underestimated it.

Fragrant Beef Rice

Beef 300 g, thinly sliced across the grain

Fragrant sesame oil 2 Tbsp

Crushed red chilli 1 tsp

Garlic 6 cloves, finely chopped

Bottled *char siew* sauce 2 Tbsp

Uncooked rice 2½ cups, washed and thoroughly drained

Chicken stock (see page 158) 3½ cups

Salt 1 tsp or to taste

Screwpine (*pandan*) leaves 4, washed and knotted

Fresh shiitake or button mushrooms 100 g, thickly sliced

Sliced spring onions (scallions) (optional) sufficient to garnish

- Combine beef, sesame oil, crushed chilli, garlic, and *char siew* sauce and mix thoroughly. Set aside.
- Put rice, chicken stock, salt and screwpine leaves into rice cooker. Stir to dissolve salt and put lid on. Turn on rice cooker and leave to cook.
- As soon as rice cooker switches to the "keep warm" mode, remove lid and put mushrooms over hot rice in an even layer. Add beef in an even layer over mushrooms and immediately put lid back on. Leave to steam for 15 minutes more, then switch off rice cooker.
- Stir rice gently to combine with beef and mushrooms. Serve garnished with sliced spring onions, if desired, crushed chillies or sliced fresh red chillies, and a drizzle of light soy sauce and sesame oil, if you like.

To Prepare: **10 minutes** To Cook: **30 minutes** Serves: **4**

This is a very simple and extremely forgiving recipe so it doesn't much matter what type of chilli you use. The important thing is for it to be hot and intensely flavoured, so don't be shy with the garlic. The crushed chilli I use is from Thailand and is generously salted so you may not need to add salt. Taste before seasoning. If you can't get this, any crushed hot dried chilli will do. Serve with white rice and cucumber slices for a simple but satisfying dinner.

Garlic Chilli Chicken

Garlic 8 cloves, finely chopped

Thai chilli flakes 4 tsp or to taste

Chicken on the bone 1 kg, cut into approximately 5-cm chunks

Water 2 Tbsp

Salt ½ tsp or to taste

Sugar (optional) a pinch

White vinegar or lime juice 2 tsp or to taste

- Heat 3–4 Tbsp oil in a pan over medium heat and add garlic and chilli. Stir until fragrant, taking care not to burn spices.
- Add chicken chunks and increase heat. Stir and turn chicken chunks over until brown.
- Reduce heat to minimum and put on lid. Stir chicken often to prevent sticking and burning. If necessary, add the water to prevent burning.
- Keep cooking with the lid on, until chicken is done and coated with chilli. This should take no more than 20 minutes in total.
- Taste and season with salt, sugar and vinegar or lime juice. Dish out and serve.

To Prepare: **10 minutes** To Cook: **20 minutes** Serves: **4**

No, they're not nymphs but they look almost pretty enough to be. To "butterfly"prawns, make an incision down the back, almost all the way through to the underside, but don't cut right through. Remove the dark vein and flatten the prawn out. All done. This is delectable, looks impressive enough for a dinner party starter and makes a wonderfully seductive supper for two as well. Imagine feeding your lover spears of asparagus with your fingers, late at night, in bed. Who knows where that could lead?

Nymphs Afloat

Slender green asparagus 100 g, trim about 5-cm off the bottom

Large prawns 2, butterflied, deveined, shell and head left intact

Prepared garlic butter 1 scant Tbsp, softened at room temperature

Sour cream 1 Tbsp

Salt to taste omit if garlic butter is highly seasoned

White pepper to taste

- Turn on your toaster oven and set for 15 minutes.
- Arrange asparagus in an even layer on a heatproof ceramic dish that fits into your toaster oven.
- Lay the well-drained prawns across the asparagus in any fashion you like. I like to lay them cut side up, pointing in opposite directions like the Pisces symbol (but that's just me).
- Combine the garlic butter and sour cream and spoon over the prawns and asparagus, putting more over the cut in the prawns. Sprinkle evenly with salt and pepper.
- When there are 10 minutes left on the toaster timer, slide in the dish and grill until timer goes off. Do not overcook.
- Remove dish from toaster oven. Take to bed alone or with a lover and a bottle of Sauvignon Blanc. Yes, things could get messy, but that's the whole point... isn't it?

To Prepare: **5 minutes** To Cook: **10 minutes** Serves: **1–2**

Float this way, baby...

The beer gives terrific flavour and aroma and seems to tenderise and moisten the meat as well. This is my solace when I crave a fried chicken fix but cringe at the thought of assaulting my hips with all that fat. Pine no more—this hits the spot but spares your waistline. Use ready cut chicken portions to save time. Nothing goes better with this than mashed potato and coleslaw or a green salad. Go on, sink your teeth into that golden, crackling skin; you know you want to....

Oven-fried Beer Chicken

Frying chicken portions 1 kg, cleaned, drained

Light beer ½ cup, free of foam

Garlic powder 2 levelled tsp

Sugar 2 levelled tsp

Salt 1 levelled tsp or to taste

White pepper 1 levelled tsp

Plain (all-purpose) flour sufficient to coat chicken

- Preheat oven at 230°C. Combine the chicken, beer, garlic powder, sugar, salt and pepper in a large bowl and mix thoroughly with your hands, rubbing the seasonings well into the chicken. If you have time, marinate for 15 minutes. If not, just proceed to the next step.
- Remove chicken pieces from marinade and coat all around with flour. Shake off excess flour and place chicken pieces skin side up on a rack set inside a roasting tray. Put tray in oven and bake for 15 minutes.
- Lower heat to 180°C and turn chicken pieces over to brown other side. Bake for another 10–15 minutes. Chicken should be cooked through by then. To be sure, test the thickest part of the largest piece with a fork–there should be no blood at the bone and cooking juices should be clear.
- When done, remove from oven and serve immediately.

To Prepare: **10 minutes** To Cook: **25–30 minutes** Serves: **4**

This is based on the Portuguese dish, pork with clams *cataplana*. *Cataplana* is both a stew and a special hinged cooking pot resembling a clam. Legend has it that this dish was invented by the Portuguese to test the faith of Jews who had converted to Christianity. Nasty things, inquisitions. The fall out in this case, though, is something I'm glad for. This luscious stew needs nothing more than boiled new potatoes drizzled with olive oil and sprinkled with salt, to make a meal that pleases both the eyes and the palate.

Portuguese-style Pork with Clams

Olive oil 5 Tbsp (don't skimp on it; it adds flavour)

Pork tenderloin or fillet 500 g, cut into small cubes

Streaky bacon 2 rashers, diced

Onion 1, medium, peeled and coarsely chopped

Garlic 6 cloves, peeled and minced

Tomatoes 2, medium, cut into large dice

Chilli flakes 1½ levelled tsp

Vinho Verde, white vermouth or white wine 1 cup

Water or chicken stock (see page 158) ½ cup

Clams in brine 1 can, about 370 g, drained

Salt ½ levelled tsp or to taste

Fresh coriander (cilantro) ¼ cup, coarsely chopped

Fruity extra virgin olive oil sufficient to drizzle

- Heat olive oil in a frying pan or deep pan over high heat. When hot, brown the pork well. Remove from pan, reserving oil. Set pork aside.
- Add bacon to pan and when crisp, add onion and garlic. Cook, stirring often, until fragrant and onions are transparent.
- Add tomatoes to pan and stir until tomatoes go limp. Add chilli flakes and wine and boil vigorously until wine is almost completely evaporated.
- Add water or stock, stir well, bring to the boil, then lower heat and return pork to the pan. Stir well, then add drained clams. Simmer until pork is done and clams are heated through. This shouldn't take more than 3–5 minutes. Season to taste and turn off heat.
- Garnish with coriander leaves and a drizzle of extra virgin olive oil. Serve with peeled and boiled potatoes.

To Prepare: **10 minutes** To Cook: **25 minutes** Serves: **4**

This is supposedly Straits Chinese in origin but then again, who knows? Whoever, however; the contrast of firm juicy prawns against the velvety smooth creaminess and peppery bite of the sauce is pure heaven. This is good with white rice or as a nibble, with beer. Straits Chinese matriarchs caution against eating this before retiring, as a night of tossing and turning restlessly in bed would ensue. I could think of far worse things then a restless night though, especially if you have company as delectable as this dish.

Prawns in Peppery Coconut Cream

- Heat oil in a deep pan over medium-high heat and fry prawns until just cooked. Remove from pan and set aside.
- Remove most of the oil from pan, reserving about 1 Tbsp and return to heat again. When hot, pour in coconut milk and add all other ingredients except onion and cucumber. Stir over medium heat until thick. Taste and adjust seasoning if necessary.
- Return prawns to the pan and turn off heat. Add onion and cucumber and mix well.
- Serve immediately.

Vegetable oil ½ cup

Medium prawns 500 g, peeled, deveined, tails left intact

Thick coconut milk ¾ cup

Large tamarind slices 2

Coarse black pepper ½ levelled tsp

Chilli flakes ½ levelled tsp

Salt ¾ levelled tsp

Sugar ¾ levelled tsp

Onion (optional) 1, medium, sliced thinly

Cucumber (optional) ½, small, discard core and shred coarsely

To Prepare: **20 minutes** To Cook: **10 minutes** Serves: **4**

This is so comforting, so warming and just the thing to cook and eat on a rainy night. If that's not enough, it's also surprisingly virtuous for something so satisfying. What little fat you'll find here is heart friendly. Even the sight of this, sitting prettily in the bowl as it gently wafts savoury and fragrant steam in your face, is so uplifting. Get the freshest salmon and the most vibrant greens you can. With such a simple recipe, you really won't be able to mask ingredients that are not up to scratch.

Salmon and Noodles in Ginger Broth

Water 8 cups

Fresh ginger 8-cm length, scraped and thickly sliced

Bottled soba sauce 6 Tbsp

Granulated chicken stock 4 levelled tsp

Salt 1½ tsp

Sugar 1½ tsp

Salmon fillet 8 thin, broad slices, about 50 g per slice

Thin dried egg noodles 8 small coils, about 300 g

Your favourite Asian greens 100 g, washed, draind and cut according to preference

Bird's eye chillies (optional) 2–3, very thinly sliced

- Combine water, ginger, soba sauce, granulated stock, salt and sugar in a pot and bring to the boil. Lower heat to minimum, cover and leave to simmer while you tend to the other ingredients.
- Fill a deep pot with enough water to blanch the noodles and vegetables.
- Heat about a tablespoon oil in a heavy pan and when smoking, very quickly sear the salmon slices (in two lots) on each side. The salmon should be rare inside. Keep the heat high and don't crowd the pan when you do this or the temperature of the pan will dip and the salmon will start losing its natural juices and turn soggy.
- When the water boils, quickly blanch the noodles and greens, taking care not to overcook.
- Place some noodles and greens in each serving bowl. Top each bowl with 2 salmon slices and ladle the steaming soup over. Scatter some chilli on top for those who want it and serve immediately.

To Prepare: **10 minutes** To Cook: **10 minutes** Serves: **4**

spicy, garlicky mo

This is very punchy, very savoury and a pleasure to eat, as the crunchy garlic bits contrast to spectacular effect, with the tender, juicy eggplant. I personally double the amount of chillies but I understand that not everyone has similarly suicidal tendencies. Adjust according to your personal level of masochism.

Spicy Eggplant with Crispy Garlic

- Put a medium-sized pot of water to boil.
- Cook eggplant for about 3 minutes in the rapidly boiling water, then remove and immediately rinse under tap water to stop cooking process. Drain well.
- Put well drained eggplant in a bowl and gently but thoroughly combine with everything else except coriander.
- Transfer to a serving dish and sprinkle coriander over.
- Serve with fried or grilled fish or chicken and white rice, or toss through blanched fine egg noodles and drizzle with toasted sesame oil.

Long purple eggplant (aubergine/brinjal) 2, medium, split lengthwise and cut into largish chunks

Bird's eye chillies 4–5, or 2 regular fresh red chillies, finely chopped

Coarsely chopped garlic 1 Tbsp, fry until crisp and reserve 3 tsp of oil to add to the cooked eggplant

Lime juice 1 Tbsp or to taste

Fish sauce 1–1½ Tbsp

Sugar ½ tsp

Chopped coriander (cilantro) leaves sufficient to garnish

To Prepare: **10 minutes** To Cook: **3 minutes** Serves: **4**

Smelt is supposedly a first cousin of salmon but hey, you can't choose your relatives. I have nothing against salmon but this is the fish for me. It's such a pity that smelt is not trendy enough to be on restaurant menus. Fry it really crisp so you can crunch right through the bones and devour it from the tip of its very delicate snout to the end of its very delectable tail. Serve with haphazardly mashed potatoes seasoned generously with salt.

Crispy Smelt with Oriental Green Sauce

Vegetable oil ½ cup

Plain (all-purpose) flour sufficient to coat fish

Salt ½ levelled tsp

White pepper ½ levelled tsp

Smelt 8 (total weight 400 g), gutted, washed well and drained

Oriental Green Sauce

Spring onion (scallion) tops (the green part) ½ cup, chopped

Toasted sesame seeds 2 levelled Tbsp

Light vegetable oil 2 Tbsp

Fragrant sesame oil 1 Tbsp

Freshly squeezed lime juice 4–6 Tbsp

Light soy sauce 1 Tbsp

Garlic 1 clove, peeled

Sugar 1 levelled tsp or to taste

Salt ½ levelled tsp or to taste

Prepared wasabi paste 1½tsp

- Put all sauce ingredients into a blender and blend to a very smooth, thick liquid.
- Pour into a jar or non-reactive container, cover and set aside.
- Heat oil in a wok or pan over medium-high heat. Combine flour, salt and pepper on a large plate. Roll 4 fish in flour and dust off excess.
- Lower fish into hot oil. After about 3 minutes, turn over. Fry on both sides, turning often to ensure fish is evenly crisp and golden. Fish must be crispy enough to crunch through numerous tiny bones. Drain on kitchen paper. Repeat with the remaining fish.
- Serve with boiled and salted potatoes, and Oriental Green Sauce.

To Prepare: **20 minutes** To Cook: **10 minutes** Serves: **2**

So sumptuous, it migh

Just the colour of this soup wreaks havoc with the imagination. How can you look at this and not think of bull fights and matadors, scarlet lips and throbbing pulses, sultry, searing evenings and swooning damsels? Pardon me; what I really meant to say was, fresh, vibrant, deeply savoury and bursting with sunny Mediterranean flavour. But I was talking about the soup, honestly! Serve with sliced crusty baguette dipped in fruity extra virgin olive oil, for a light supper, or alone as an elegant starter.

Scarlet Soup

- Heat olive oil in a pot and gently brown the garlic and ginger. When fragrant, add red pepper and cook gently for about 5 minutes.
- Add carrots and beetroot and stir for 3 minutes or so. Put lid on, reduce heat to minimum and cook for about 6 minutes.
- Open lid and pour in vermouth. Increase heat and cook until liquid is almost evaporated. Add chicken stock and bring to the boil.
- Remove from heat and pour soup into a heatproof blender, or use an immersion blender if you have one (see Note on page 41). Purée until smooth as a baby's bottom. Pour back into pot and return to heat gently until simmering. Season to taste.
- Serve in individual bowls garnished with diced beetroot and drizzled with extra virgin olive oil if you like.

Olive oil 3 Tbsp

Garlic 6 fat cloves, chopped

Ginger 5-cm length, peeled and minced

Red bell pepper (capsicum) 1½ cups (about 150 g), peeled and diced

Carrot 1 cup (about 50 g), peeled and diced

Fresh beetroot 1 cup (about 50 g), peeled and diced

Red vermouth (Martini Rosso) ½ cup

Chicken stock (see page 158) 2½ cups

Salt to taste

White pepper to taste

Extra virgin olive oil sufficient to drizzle

Extra uncooked fresh beetroot (optional) sufficient to garnish, diced

make you blush

To Prepare: **10 minutes** To Cook: **20 minutes** Serves: **4**

Tuna is one of the easiest fish to cook. If you're really rushed, you can do away with cooking and have it au naturel, which is probably the best way to eat it, if it's truly fresh. With its meaty yet meltingly tender texture, how can one not fall madly in love? This recipe doesn't mess around too much with it. Just stiffly fresh tuna, innocent of even salt, momentarily singed in a blisteringly hot pan, served with steaming, savoury rice. On the side, a spicy-cool cucumber, chilli and ginger relish to keep things humming along.

Singed Tuna with Savoury Rice and Cucumber Relish

Fragrant sesame oil 2 Tbsp

Garlic 3 cloves, peeled and minced

Fresh peeled ginger 6 broad, thin slices

Jasmine rice 1½ cups, uncooked, washed and drained

Chicken stock (see page 158) 2¼ cups

Skinned, trimmed tuna fillet 300–400 g, get your fishmonger to prepare the tuna for you

Black and white sesame seeds 1 Tbsp each

Fresh coriander (cilantro) leaves (optional) sufficient to garnish

Relish

Cucumber ½, medium, seeded, peeled and coarsely chopped

Fresh red chillies 2

Lime juice 1 Tbsp

Light flavoured oil 1 Tbsp

Garlic 2 cloves

Fresh ginger 3 broad, thin slices

Salt 1 levelled tsp

Sugar (optional) 1 levelled tsp

Note: Light flavoured oil refers to oils that have no distinctive or strong smell and taste. Examples of light flavoured oils that are readily available include sunflower, safflower, canola, soy or grapeseed.

- Heat the sesame oil in a small pot and fry garlic and ginger until fragrant and limp. Add the rice and stir until coated with oil. Pour in the stock and bring to the boil, uncovered.
- When the stock has almost evaporated and little holes appear on the surface of the rice, cover the pot securely and reduce heat to minimum. Leave to cook for 10 minutes.
- While rice cooks, heat a tablespoon of oil in a non-stick pan until smoking. Coat tuna fillet with sesame seeds evenly, then sear for about ½ minute on each side. Don't overcook. Set aside.
- Combine all ingredients for relish except for cucumber, in a blender and blend until slightly chunky. Fold in chopped cucumber and taste. Add a little salt if necessary. Rice should be cooked by now. Turn off heat and leave to settle for 10 minutes.
- When ready to serve, put some rice on each plate. Slice thickly across the tuna fillet and lay on the plates. Spoon the relish around the rice and tuna. Garnish with coriander leaves, extra sesame oil and serve.

To Prepare: 15 minutes **To Cook:** 20 minutes **Serves:** 2

Incongruous as it may sound, this really is a divine combination. The richness of the fish is beautifully offset by the slightly sharp and fruity dressing, with the garlic adding a bit of punch. This is good enough and looks beautiful enough to grace the Christmas dinner table. And oh my God! It is so very much easier and quicker than turkey. With buttered broad egg noodles or boiled potatoes, a simple green salad and a glass of dry New Zealand Riesling, you would have all you need for a truly memorable meal.

Salmon Fillet in Warm Almond, Berry and Garlic Vinaigrette

- Combine all dressing ingredients in a screw top jar and shake vigorously until salt and sugar are completely dissolved. Refrigerate until needed.
- Heat 1 Tbsp oil in a large heavy-based frying pan. When really hot, put in the fillets, skin side up and cook on high heat for about 1 minute.
- Turn over and cook other side on high heat for about another minute. Lift fillets onto individual dinner plates.
- Add a little more oil to the pan and gently cook the garlic until limp and fragrant. Add chilli flakes, stir for a minute or so then pour in vinaigrette. Stir and heat through. Season to taste. Turn off heat.
- Pour warm vinaigrette over each fillet and garnish with lemon or lime wedge or slice before serving.

Vegetable oil 1Tbsp

Salmon fillets with skin 4, each weighing 150–200 g

Garlic 4 cloves, peeled and minced

Chilli flakes ½ levelled tsp

Salt ½ levelled tsp, or to taste

Dressing Ingredients

Unsweetened cranberry juice ½ cup

Light flavoured oil ⅓ cup

Lemon juice 1 Tbsp

Dried cranberries 1 levelled Tbsp, finely chopped

Shallots 1 levelled Tbsp, finely chopped

Fresh parsley 1 levelled Tbsp, finely chopped

Toasted almonds 2 levelled tsp, finely ground

Red pepper or chilli flakes ½ tsp

Garlic powder ½ levelled tsp

Salt 2 levelled tsp or to taste

Sugar 3 levelled tsp or to taste

To Prepare: **15 minutes** To Cook: **10 minutes** Serves: **4**

Teaser? Because the dainty portion leaves me still hungry and wanting more. Hmm, are we still talking about appetisers? The tuna is dipped into the condiment of choice before eating and this is a great way to inject some fun at the dinner table. This makes an excellent starter for one or a cosy supper or snack for two, if you could actually be convinced to share it. Ensure the tuna is of sashimi grade and extremely fresh. Some sticky Japanese rice and miso soup would turn this into a light dinner for two.

Tuna Teaser

Sashimi-grade tuna fillet 150 g, chilled

Ponzu (Japanese citrus vinegar) ½ small shot glass

Japanese soy sauce ½ small shot glass

Dried *shiso* leaf ½ small shot glass

Prepared wasabi paste preferred amount

Note: Also known as Japanese mint or perilla, *shiso* comes in two varieties, green and purple. The purple variety is more pungent. Although *shiso* is a type of mint, it tastes more like cinnamon, with hints of citrus and coriander.

- Slice the tuna as thick or thin as you like, across the grain, using a very sharp knife.
- Pile the tuna onto a plate and surround with the condiments.
- Get a pair of chopsticks and tuck in immediately, before your sashimi-mad partner gets wind of what you're up to and catches up.

To Prepare: 5 minutes **Serves:** 1–2

Drinks

If you're looking for mere liquids that will wash down food or quench your thirst, you won't find them here. But if its incredibly, addictively chic cocktails that will be a hit at parties, and earn you a guest list that will beat the hottest bar in town hands down, come on right in! The tamer hot beverages will go perfectly with afternoon tea, paired with dessert, or a good book. A warning though: you might be compelled to keep the cocktails flowing fast and hard. Make sure your guests don't drive if they drink!

I can't decide if this is more love potion or witch's brew. Grand Marnier after dinner is lovely. You won't believe though the "alchemy" that occurs when you drop rosebuds and a stick of cinnamon into a glass of it. After a few minutes, this smells, I imagine, the way Aphrodite's boudoir might. Even the husband can't stop sniffing appreciatively at it, although he says Grand Marnier is too "girly" for him. Most importantly, just the smell of this has a curiously "reviving" effect on him. Imagine if he actually drank it. 1 part = 30 ml or 2 Tbsp.

Aphrodite's Goblet

Grand Marnier liqueur 1 part

Dried edible rosebuds 3 or 4

Cinnamon stick 5-cm length

- Pour Grand Marnier into a liqueur glass. Drop in rosebuds.
- Slide cinnamon stick in carefully amongst the rosebuds. Steep for 5 minutes.
- Let significant other sniff ever so often as you take delicate sips.
- Plan for an early (and long) night.

Better th

To Prepare: **2 minutes** Serves: **1**

love potion no. 9 – whatever that is

This is my humble ode to the Arabian Nights. I use Buderim Ginger Refresher mixer, which is really gingery and not too sweet. Rosewater is easily available from neighbourhood Indian grocery shops here. This is so refreshing and wonderful if you have overindulged at dinner and need quick relief from your discomfort. 1 part = 30 ml or 2 Tbsp.

Arabesque

- Fill a cocktail shaker with ice.
- Pour in orange juice, ginger syrup, crème de menthe and rosewater. Cap securely and shake vigorously, keeping a finger on the shaker cap.
- Pour mixture through strainer into a fluted or martini glass and top up with soda water.
- Garnish decoratively with orange peel if you like.
- Don a kaftan, stretch out on rose petal-strewn silk cushions and sip leisurely.

Ice cubes sufficient to half-fill a cocktail shaker

Unsweetened pure orange juice 2 parts

Ginger syrup 1 part

Crème de Menthe 1 part

Rosewater ½ part (about 1 Tbsp)

Soda water sufficient to top up glass

Orange peel (optional) 1 long strip, to garnish

Note: Both Crème de Menthe and rosewater are highly aromatic and distinctly flavoured. Lessen the amount used if you find it too strong.

To Prepare: **5 minutes** Serves: **1**

This is served in Morocco at all times of the day and is the single most popular drink there. A guest is never turned away without a cup and even as you enter any shop in a Moroccan *souk* or bazaar, whether or not you buy anything, you will probably be offered some. This is surprisingly refreshing despite being served hot. Mint is known to warm the body and stimulate the appetite, although which appetite is meant, remains unclear. Well, this way or the other, a little warming stimulation never did hurt anyone.

Moroccan Mint Tea

Fresh mint leaves 2 good handfuls, stems removed, washed and drained

Cube sugar 6 lumps, or use 3 Tbsp granulated sugar

Good-quality green tea 4 tea bags

Freshly boiled water sufficient to fill chosen tea pot

Note : This is excellent served after a rich and spicy meal, to soothe an overworked tummy.

- Get a teapot that will serve four generously.
- Put the mint leaves in teapot.
- Put sugar on top of mint leaves.
- Put teabags in pot and pour in hot water almost to the brim.
- Leave to steep for about 4 minutes.
- Pour a cup of tea out and then pour it back into the teapot. Repeat this about 5 or 6 times until sugar is dissolved and diffused through the tea.
- Discard teabags but leave mint leaves in pot and pour into cups or handled glasses.
- Serve immediately.

To Prepare: 8 minutes **Serves:** 4

The magic of Morocco captured in a tea cup

I love a Tom Collins every now and then and when I decided to drop in a few chunks of preserved aloe, I found that I loved it even more. The aloe plant is actually a variety of cactus, hence the name. You can easily find preserved aloe chunks in jars and packages in most supermarkets in the Asian foods section. They come in various flavours: use your favourite. I think that generally, those pickled cactus chunks would compliment most gin or vodka-based cocktails. 1 part = 30 ml or 2 Tbsp.

Cactus Collins

- Half-fill a shaker with ice and pour in gin, pickling juice, lemon juice and sugar.
- Shake well, until sugar is dissolved.
- Strain into a tall glass that's a third full of ice.
- Top up with soda water and pop in the skewered aloe chunks.
- Enjoy.

Ice sufficient to half fill cocktail shaker and chill drink

Gin 2 parts

Pickling juice 1 part, taken from preserved aloe

Lemon juice from ½ a small lemon

Fine sugar 1½ tsp (optional)

Soda water sufficient to top up glass

Preserved aloe vera cubes 4 large chunks, skewered on sharp ended cocktail stirrer

Lemon quarter slice 1, thick, to keep aloe chunks from sliding off the stirrer

To Prepare: **5 minutes** Serves: **1**

This is a grown up virgin cocktail. There's no alcohol but the fresh ginger gives it a real kick. It's hard to give exact amounts here. I love a throat-burning, gingery bite derived from a generous amount of ginger and not too much sweetness, but adjust to suit your taste. If you like it really dry, use soda water instead of lemon lime soda, or a mixture of the two. This drink is pretty enough to make me weep and who on earth could ever resist a hickey, let alone a strawberry one?

Strawberry Hickey

Ripe strawberries 8, large, rinsed, hulled and quartered

Freshly squeezed lemon juice ½ cup

Sugar ¼–½ cup

Fresh ginger 8-cm length, scraped clean, washed, and roughly chopped

Lemon lime soda or soda water 6 cups, well-chilled

- Pop the strawberries, lemon juice, sugar and ginger into the blender and blend until very smooth. You may want to strain out the strawberry seeds. Or you may not. It doesn't matter, really.
- Pour into a tall pitcher filled with very large chunks of ice. Cubes will melt too quickly and dilute the drink, causing it to separate. Not very attractive.
- Top up with lemon lime soda and stir.
- Pour into glasses and serve.

To Prepare: **10 minutes** **Serves:** **4–6**

No alcohol involved in
this feisty little baby!

Malibu has got to be my favourite liqueur. The trouble with it is it tastes so damnably good and is so terrifically refreshing that you forget you're downing alcohol. I could go through 2 or 3 of these in a blink and only realize I've had too much when my head starts to feel too big for my neck and everything suddenly seems too, too funny. The combination of coconut, lime and booze is heaven in a glass. 1 part = 30 ml or 2 Tbsp.

Coconut Toddy

- Fill a tall glass with the ice. Pour Malibu, rum, lime juice and coconut juice over ice.
- Top up with soda water and drop in lime slices. Pop in a cocktail stirrer and serve.
- *Salut*!

Ice sufficient to fill ⅓ of a tall glass

Malibu liqueur 1 part

White rum 1 part

Lime juice 1 part

Clear coconut juice with coconut pulp 2 parts

Soda water sufficient to top up glass

Calamansi lime ½, very thinly sliced

To Prepare: **5 minutes** Serves: **1**

Chai has humble origins and is drunk in Indian homes after meals to aid digestion. I was taught to make this by a Punjabi friend a very long time ago. I had the temerity to ask her if this was the real thing. She glared at me and said "My mother makes it this way, my grandmother makes it this way, so I make it this way and my daughter will make it this way." Couldn't have put it better myself. Consider this penance in a cup, for all the sinful indulging this book has seduced you into committing.

Chai

Black tea (preferably Sri Lankan tea) 4 tea bags, remove labels

Water 4 cups

Plump green cardamom pods 6, lightly crush with back of a spoon

Cinnamon stick 5-cm length

Evaporated milk ⅓ cup or adjust to taste

Sugar 3 levelled Tbsp or adjust to taste

- Combine everything except sugar in a small, heavy-bottomed pot and bring to the boil.
- As soon as the tea hits a rolling boil, turn off the heat and add sugar. Stir until sugar dissolves. Discard teabags.
- Strain into cups and serve immediately. Sip while hot.

To Prepare: **5 minutes** Serves: **2–4**

Gloomy weather,
goodbye; tropica

Short of an air ticket, this is the fastest route to the Pacific islands. Luscious mango and fragrant, juicy pineapple whizzed into a heady mix of vodka, Malibu and zesty lime. Whip up, pour into a tall glass and pop in a paper umbrella. Then imagine yourself stretched out on the beach, blue sky above, turquoise water, lapping at your feet and a host of heavenly (sun-kissed) bodies all around. Maybe this should have been called "Wet Dream in a Glass"? This recipe makes enough to fill one tall or two short tumblers. 1 part = 30 ml or 2 Tbsp.

Hula Skirt

- Put all ingredients except pineapple slices and lime slices for garnishing into a blender and blend until smooth.
- Fill chosen glass or glasses and garnish with a pineapple slice and a lime slice if desired.
- Bring glass and self to sunny balcony, stretch out and prop feet up before taking long, slow sips. Seaside vista optional and oh, so preferable.

Fresh ripe pineapple ½ cup, skinned and cubed or sliced

Fresh ripe mango ½ cup, skinned and cubed or sliced

Malibu liqueur 2 parts

Vodka 1 part

Lime juice 1 part

Ice 1–1½ cups

Pineapple slices (optional) sufficient to garnish

Lime slices (optional) sufficient to garnish

Note: You can choose to create a crusted rim on your glasses. Moisten glass rims, then dip into a saucer of castor sugar and salt mixture (made up of equal parts) before pouring in drink. The salt will add an unexpected but pleasant jolt to the drink.

sun, aloha!

To Prepare: 10 minutes **Serves: 1–2**

I have a weakness for Campari and cocktails based on it. It's the colour and beguiling grapefruit scent that get me. I named this "firefly" because the colour reminded me of a shade of Clinique lipstick I used to wear, yes, "firefly" that my husband used to go absolutely mad for. He told me once that had it not been for that particular shade of lipstick, we might not be married today. *Hmm.* 1 part=30 ml or 2 Tbsp

Firefly

Ice sufficient to half fill a cocktail shaker

Campari 1 part

Lime juice ½ part (approximately 1 Tbsp)

Cranberry juice 2 parts

Castor sugar (optional) 1 tsp

Soda water sufficient to top up glass

- Fill cocktail shaker with ice. Pour in Campari, lime juice and cranberry juice.
- Add sugar, if using, cap and shake vigorously until sugar dissolves.
- Strain into a chilled martini or fluted glass and top up with soda water.
- Garnish with red maraschino cherries or fresh or frozen cranberries, if you like.

To Prepare: **3 minutes** Serves: **1**

lose yourself in the
caffeinated, vel

You have to love the nonchalance of the Indonesians. They grow some of the best coffee in the world, then they chuck it in a cup with hot water and sugar, stir and leave before sipping ever so leisurely while the world goes by. Baristas? Coffee machines? Strainer? No, how about a gritty but delicious cup of *kopi tubruk* instead? The unexpected grittiness makes for a good joke on anyone unsuspecting but the aroma, flavour and *crema* this method produces is seriously good for any bona fide coffee lover.

Mud Coffee

Medium fine ground pure coffee (preferably Indonesian) 2 rounded tsp

Sugar 1–2 tsp

Freshly boiled hot water enough for 1 cup

- Put coffee and sugar into a tall and narrow coffee cup (to better preserve the heat of the water).
- Pour water into cup until slightly over three-quarters full Stir until sugar dissolves.
- Remove spoon from cup, cover to retain heat and leave coffee to settle for about 5 minutes.
- Serve immediately.

Note: The phrase "*kopi tubruk*" literally and strangely means "clashing coffee" in Bali, where this method of making and serving coffee originated. I call this mud coffee because of the "muddy" dregs left behind in the cup after drinking.

To Prepare: **5 minutes** Serves: **1**

They say a person has two stomachs: one for food and another for dessert. If you're the type of person who is constantly hanging up the diet bib to make room for dessert, then make sure you waste your calories on desserts that are worth your while! Most of the recipes can be prepared in advance, some days before some a few comfortable hours ahead of time for a party and some, as and when your sweet tooth starts to throb and ache and beg you to satiate it. I may as well also declare that I love chocolate, as evident from the number of recipes that feature it; never take anyone seriously when they say they don't really like chocolate.

Desserts & Baking

This is a crustless tart and a recipe borne of impatience and an undying devotion to chocolate. It's very dark, very intense but not too sweet and a surefire way to gratify your favourite chocoholic. Use dark chocolate that contains at least 50 per cent cocoa solids. I use unsweetened chocolate but semi-sweet is fine if you prefer something less intense. If you don't mind the expense, a handful of ruby bright raspberries strewn across the plate would be a beautiful touch.

Bare Bottom Chocolate Tart

Good-quality dark unsweetened chocolate 120 g, broken in pieces

Heavy or whipping cream 1 cup

Sour cream 1 cup

Sugar 1 levelled cup

Vanilla extract 1½ tsp

Eggs 3

Almonds or hazelnuts (optional) ½ cup, finely ground

Note: One 23-cm tart serves 6–8 people.

- Set oven at 160°C. Grease a 23-cm tart tin or mould thoroughly.
- Combine chocolate and heavy cream in a large, microwave- safe bowl and microwave for 1 minute on High. Remove, stir and microwave again on High for 30 seconds if mixture has not liquefied completely. Stir until completely melted and combined.
- Leave chocolate mixture to cool for about 5 minutes or until comfortably warm.
- Stir in sour cream, sugar and vanilla until well-combined and sugar has dissolved. Stir in eggs one at a time, followed by nuts, if using. Mix thoroughly but gently.
- Pour mixture into tart tin or mould and bake for 35 minutes. Remove from oven and cool at least 30 minutes before slicing.
- Serve as is or with some crème fraîche on the side.

To Prepare: **10 minutes** To Bake: **35 minutes** Makes: **one 23-cm tart**

I'll always be a dupe for anything faraway or lushly exotic. The city of Cordoba in Andalusia, Spain, once the crown jewel of the Umayyad Caliphate, was famed for its unrivalled opulence and sounds unbearably romantic. Being a cheesecake addict and an Arabian princess wannabe makes this, to me, perfection on a plate. The whipped cream swirls, crystallised rose petals and rosebuds, though strictly window dressing, add a charmingly whimsical touch to this creamy but light and intoxicatingly fragrant, Arabic-nuanced cheesecake.

Cheesecake Cordoba

1 store-bought round pound/sponge/butter cake 300 g, about 20 cm in diameter and 5 cm in height

Soft cream cheese 350 g, softened at room temperature

Sour cream 150 g

Eggs 2

Fine sugar 100 g

Vanilla extract 1 tsp

Rose extract ½ tsp

Orange zest grated from 1 orange, avoid the white pith

Rose syrup 1–2 Tbsp

Whipped cream or commercial frosting to anchor rose buds or petals (optional)

Dried edible rose buds or crystallised rose petals to decorate as you wish (optional)

- Preheat oven at 160°C. Line a 12-hole muffin tin with paper cases. Slice cake horizontally into 3 layers. Cut out 12 rounds from the 3 layers, using a 4-cm cookie cutter. Put one round into the base of each paper case and press down lightly. Prick each round a few times with a fork.
- Combine cheese, sour cream, eggs, sugar, vanilla extract, rose extract, orange zest and rose syrup in a large bowl. Gently whisk until smooth and free of lumps.
- Divide mixture evenly amongst the cake-lined paper cases. Place tray into oven and bake for 20 minutes. Turn off oven and open oven door slightly, but leave cheesecakes to sit for about 30 minutes. Remove from oven and cool completely.
- Decorate with piped whipped cream or commercial frosting and rosebuds or petals if you wish.

Note: The colour of the finished cheesecake will depend on the amount and the colour intensity of the rose syrup.

Crystallised Rose Petals

Fresh, clean and unblemished rose petals of your preferred colour

Egg white 1, lightly beaten

Castor (superfine) sugar as needed

Fine tea strainer or small sieve

Fine-tipped tweezers

Non-stick baking paper

Cake rack 1

- Ensure the surface of the rose petals are dry. Using the tweezers, dip each petal into egg white and allow excess to drip off. Using the strainer, dust both sides of rose petal generously and evenly with castor sugar, over the baking paper. Transfer rose petals to the cake rack and allow to dry. This can take up to a day, depending on the weather and humidity.
- If it's a damp or rainy day, dry the rose petals in a very cool oven heated to about 80°C for about 45 minutes.

Note: Store rose petals in an airtight container in layers ,separated by non-stick baking paper and consume within 2 weeks. Do not keep in the refrigerator or they will go limp. Make sure the roses you use for the crystallised rose petals have not been sprayed with chemical pesticides and when buying, specify that you want food-grade roses.

To Prepare: **15 minutes** To Bake: **20 minutes** Makes: **12 cupcakes**

These are perfect when it's late afternoon and dinner is still some way off but your tummy is protesting. They're incredibly easy to stir up and look amazingly like miniature bagels when done, though they're softer and taste better than any bagel I've ever had. Add a pot of coffee or tea and you've got a cosy and intimate Sunday afternoon at home to catch up and connect with your Significant Other before the mad rush starts again on Monday morning.

Chocolate Cranberry Rings

Plain (all-purpose) flour 1¼ cups

Baking soda ½ levelled tsp

Cream of tartar 1 levelled tsp

Instant yeast granules 1 levelled tsp

Sugar ¼–⅓ cup

Dried cranberries ⅓ cup

Dark chocolate (chunks or chips) ⅔ cup

Egg 1

Unsweetened plain yoghurt 2 Tbsp

Water ½ cup

Vanilla extract 1 tsp

- Set oven at 200°C. Thoroughly grease a mini bundt tray.
- Thoroughly combine in a large mixing bowl the flour, baking soda and cream of tartar. Add yeast, sugar, cranberries and chocolate. Mix thoroughly.
- Whisk together in a separate bowl the egg, yoghurt, water and vanilla. Pour liquid mixture into bowl of dry ingredients and stir gently until well mixed. Put 2 generous tablespoons of batter into each bundt cup, spreading evenly around the funnel and taking care not to get batter on the funnel.
- Bake for 10 minutes, then lower temperature to 180°C. Bake another 5 minutes. Remove from oven and leave to cool in tray for about 3 minutes before turning out onto a cooling rack.
- Curl up on the couch with your favourite companion, a plateful of these and a cup of coffee or tea within reach.

To Prepare: **15 minutes** To Bake: **15 minutes** Makes: **6–8 rings**

Look fashionable while eating!

Syllabub is a wine-spiked, sweetened whipped cream. It takes all of 5 minutes to make, is endlessly permutable and is a dessert you can make hours ahead, chill and forget about while you do the rest of your dinner party menu. Did I say "dinner party?" This is just the kind of dessert you might want to serve dinner guests. It's unbearably chic, and sparkles with the sharp fruitiness of the plum wine and the intoxicating floral notes of jasmine green tea. Of course, you could always whip this up as an indulgent treat, just for the two of you.

Plum Wine and Green Tea Syllabub

Japanese plum wine like Choya 100 ml, chilled

Very finely ground jasmine green tea 3 tsp

Castor (superfine) sugar 3 levelled Tbsp or to taste

Whipping cream 200 ml, well-chilled

- In a large bowl, combine plum wine, green tea and sugar and whisk until sugar dissolves.
- Pour in the whipping cream and continue whisking until soft peaks form and hold their shape. Do not overwhisk or an 'oily' taste will develop. If overwhisked, whipping cream will separate and turn buttery.
- Divide mixture amongst four liqueur or shot glasses and chill thoroughly before serving.
- I'll let you in on a little secret; if you freeze this for 3 hours, you'll have the easiest, most wicked ice cream ever. *Shhhhhh*!

To Prepare: **5 minutes** Serves: **2–4**

Remember Hansel and Gretel? Had that witch baked better gingerbread, those two might have never escaped her clutches. Fresh ginger gives this cake a brighter, zestier flavour than dried and the deep, mysterious smoky tones of cocoa only add to its appeal. If you can't get muscovado or molasses sugar, any soft dark sugar will do. If you like gingerbread, this will make you swoon. In medieval Europe, ginger was believed to inflame the passions and was so prized, a pound of it was equal to the value of a sheep! Thank goodness it's a bit cheaper now. For a whimsical presentation, slice loaf thickly, then stamp out shapes with a cookie cutter.

Fresh Ginger Loaf

Fresh ginger 50 g (about ⅓ cup), scraped and sliced

Water ½ cup

Plain (all-purpose) flour 200 g (about 2 cups)

Baking soda 1 tsp

Cream of tartar 2 tsp

Pure cocoa powder 1 levelled Tbsp

Butter at room temperature 150 g (about 1 cup)

Muscovado or dark brown sugar 100 g (about ¾ cup)

Molasses sugar 100 g (about ¾ cup)

Ground nutmeg or cinnamon 1 levelled tsp

Eggs 2

Vanilla extract 2 tsp

White or apple cider vinegar 1 Tbsp

Note: One 23-cm loaf serves about 6 people.

- Preheat oven at 180°C. Grease and flour a 10-cm by 23-cm loaf tin.
- Process ginger and ½ cup water in a blender until very smooth. Set aside. Combine flour, baking soda, cream of tartar and cocoa in a large bowl and sift twice. Set aside.
- Cream the butter, sugars and nutmeg or cinnamon until fluffy. Whisk in eggs one at a time, adding vanilla with the second egg.
- Fold in flour in two lots, ensuring there are no pockets of unmixed flour. Gently stir in the processed ginger and vinegar. When you add the vinegar, the batter will foam up slightly. This is a reaction between the baking soda and the acid in the vinegar and it will lighten the cake batter.
- Quickly scrape the batter into the tin and bake for about 35 minutes. When it is 30 minutes into the baking, test with a skewer. If it comes out clean, the cake is done. The middle of the cake may sink a little because of the high moisture content of the batter. However, the cake will be very tender and airy when you cut it.
- When cake is done, remove from oven and leave to cool at least 20 minutes before cutting. Serve thickly sliced and generously dusted with icing sugar. Wash it down with strong milky tea.

To Prepare: **15 minutes** To Bake: **35 minutes** Makes: **one 23-cm loaf**

Honeyed, mellow mouthfuls

Did you really think you could evade temptation so ungodly in a book such as this? Such depravity might have prompted Caligula into a hair shirt, had he eaten it. The frosting heroically defies sweltering temperatures and holds its precipitous peaks, out of the refrigerator, at midday, in June, in the tropics! I dare say it would hold up at the very periphery of hell. I can recommend it no higher; already I tread precariously on the edge of blasphemy. All those not seriously in deepest, darkest, chocolate bondage, look away. We wouldn't want to upset anyone.

Infernal Chocolate Brownies

Unsweetened dark chocolate 200 g, broken into pieces

Butter 200 g (about 1⅓ cup), softened at room temperature

Fine sugar 200 g (about 1⅓ cup)

Eggs 3

Vanilla extract 2 tsp

Self-raising flour 100 g (about 1 cup)

Frosting

Nutella chocolate spread 6 rounded Tbsp

Pure unsweetened cocoa powder 4 levelled Tbsp

- Preheat oven at 180°C. Line a 20-cm by 30-cm baking tray with kitchen foil and grease the foil.
- Combine chocolate and butter in a large microwave-safe bowl and microwave for 1 minute on High. Remove, stir and microwave again on High for 30 seconds if mixture has not liquefied completely. Stir until completely melted and combined. Set aside to cool slightly, or until comfortably warm but still liquid.
- In another bowl, whisk together the sugar, eggs and vanilla until sugar dissolves. While whisking, pour chocolate mixture in. When combined, gently but thoroughly whisk in the flour. Pour batter into lined tray and bake for 20 minutes. Remove from oven and leave to cool.
- To make frosting, put Nutella into a large bowl and sift over the cocoa. Whisk until smooth and spreadable. If not using immediately, cover and set aside.
- When brownie is completely cool, spread frosting over and let it set before cutting.

Note: One 30-cm cake serves about 4 people. Serve as is cut into small squares or bars or serve larger pieces with a scoop of good vanilla ice cream and a cup of espresso, for an insanely indulgent dessert. Recommended penance: run 5 km the next day.

To Prepare: 15 minutes **To Bake:** 20 minutes **Makes:** one 30-cm cake

You really could make any flavour of boozy jelly. Use your favourite cocktails as inspiration for flavour combination–vodka and cranberry, gin and lime, tequila and orange. Getting the picture? If you don't want to fiddle with whole coconuts, just get 300 ml of canned coconut juice with coconut pulp and you can get on with the business of covertly getting your chosen victim(s) drunk on this luscious-tasting but innocuous-looking jelly, that much faster.

Malibu, Coconut and Lime Jellies

Unflavoured ice jelly crystals or powder 1 sachet (about 25 g)

Sugar ½ cup

Screwpine leaves 2, knotted

Water 450 ml (about 2¼ cup)

Clear coconut juice from 1 young coconut 300 ml (about 1½ cup), scoop out and reserve flesh, or use canned coconut juice that has pulp

Lime juice 50 ml (about ¼ cup)

Malibu liqueur 200 ml (about 1 cup)

Note: Omit screwpine leaves if they are unavailable. Screwpine flavouring extracts are usually a poor substitute for the real thing.

- Combine jelly crystals, sugar, screwpine leaves and water in a pot. Bring to the boil, stirring until sugar dissolves.
- When mixture boils and sugar and jelly crystals have dissolved completely, add coconut and lime juices and Malibu and stir. Taste and add more sugar if necessary. Turn off heat.
- Put coconut flesh into one large or several individual jelly moulds. Remove screwpine leaves and pour the jelly mix into mould(s). Leave to cool, then refrigerate to set until firm and as cold as you like it.
- To unmould, dip base and sides of mould(s) into very hot water for a few seconds. If using a large mould, put a large plate over mould and carefully turn over onto plate. Jelly should plop out easily in one piece.
- I like to serve this jelly at the end of a spicy south-east Asian, particularly, Indonesian or Thai meal.

To Prepare: **10 minutes** Makes: **8 small jellies or 1 large jelly**

Eat, whi

I made this one night at 11.20 pm, when a sudden craving for chocolate struck the husband. This cake is really delicious, moist, rises superbly and is very quick and easy to put together. You won't be disappointed, I think. We were so driven by chocolate lust because of the incredible chocolate aroma wafting out of the oven that we pounced on it the moment it came out!

Midnight Craving Chocolate Cake

Plain (all-purpose) flour 1½ cups

Baking soda 1 tsp

Cream of tartar 2 levelled tsp

Instant yeast granules 2 levelled tsp

Unsweetened pure cocoa powder ⅓ cup

Soft brown sugar 1¼ cup

Light vegetable oil ⅔ cup

Water ⅔ cup

White vinegar 1 Tbsp

Vanilla extract 1 tsp

Egg 1

Mini dark chocolate chips ½ cup (or as much as you like)

- Preheat oven at 180°C. Grease a 20-cm square cake tin.
- Thoroughly combine flour, baking soda and cream of tartar in a large bowl. Add yeast, cocoa and sugar and whisk together until combined.
- Add oil, water, vinegar, vanilla and egg. Whisk until yeast granules are no longer visible.
- Pour batter into cake tin, scatter chocolate chips over batter and bake for 15 minutes. Reduce heat to 165°C and continue baking for another 15 minutes.
- Test with a skewer; it should come out from the centre of cake with a little cake sticking to it.
- Remove from oven, wait as long as you can for it to cool. Dive in, face first, before going to bed, appeased.

Note: One 20-cm cake serves about 4 people.

the clock strikes twelve...

To Prepare: **10 minutes** To Bake: **30 minutes** Makes: **one 20-cm cake**

This is chocolate mousse and tiramisu for the indolent and chocolate dependent amongst us who are still a bit too discriminating to rip open a chocolate bar and savagely relieve ourselves. You won't believe how easy this is until you try it. Rich, dark, velvety, and oh, so deeply satisfying. Got you now? The Ritter Sport brand of chocolate is perfect for this as their dark chocolate is the ideal balance of chocolate intensity and subtle sweetness. Feel free though, to use your preferred brand. Italian lady finger biscuits are best, if you can find them.

Moussamisu

Dark chocolate (50%) 100 g, broken into squares

Pure dairy whipping cream 200 ml (about 1 cup), well chilled

Lady finger biscuits 6

Tia Maria or Kahlua liqueur 6 Tbsp

Unsweetened liquid good-quality black coffee 6 Tbsp, cooled

Extra dark grated chocolate sufficient amount to garnish

- Put chocolate into a clean, dry microwave-safe bowl and microwave on High for 1 minute. Remove bowl, stir and microwave on High for another 30 seconds. Stir until chocolate is completely melted. Set aside to cool slightly.
- Whisk cold cream in a large bowl until fluffy and standing in soft peaks. This should take about 2 minutes' worth of vigorous and continuous hand-whisking. Gently but thoroughly combine the cooled but still liquid chocolate and whisked cream. Cover and refrigerate.
- Break lady fingers into halves or quarters and place in a 1-litre capacity bowl, or divide the lady fingers amongst 4 short glasses or ramekins. Lady fingers should fit the base of bowl, glasses or ramekins snugly. Combine liqueur and coffee and pour evenly over lady fingers.
- Remove chocolate and cream mixture from refrigerator and spoon over the liqueur-soaked lady fingers. Gently bang the bowl, glasses or ramekins on counter to remove air pockets. Refrigerate to chill for 2 hours.
- Garnish with grated dark chocolate and serve immediately.

To Prepare: 10 minutes **Serves:** 2–4

Nutty,
crunchy goodness

These are biscotti, flavoured differently, and shaped and cut smaller than commercially-produced biscotti. They look quite stunning, thanks to the chartreuse-green chunks of pistachio they're studded with. These are equally good for nibbling with coffee, tea or dessert wines. Almonds would be just as nice, if you can't get pistachios. They smell and taste heavenly but best of all, don't contain much fat. I usually make a double batch–they go very fast!

Orange and Pistachio Fingers

Plain (all-purpose) flour 150 g (about 1½ cups)

Baking powder ½ tsp

Egg 1

Fine sugar 75 g (about ½ cup)

Vanilla extract 1 tsp

Grated orange zest from 1 small orange, avoid white pith

Whole shelled pistachios 50 g (about ½ cup)

- Preheat oven at 180°C. Lightly grease a baking sheet. Whisk flour and baking powder together in a bowl.
- In a separate, large bowl, whisk egg, sugar, vanilla and orange zest until creamy.
- Add flour mixture and pistachios to egg and vanilla mixture and knead gently until a dough forms. Don't be tempted to add more flour; just flour your hands so you can handle the dough more easily without it sticking to your hands.
- Shape dough into a flattened log, about 25-cm by 10-cm and place on lined baking sheet. Place sheet on the oven's middle rack and bake for 15 minutes. Remove log from oven and cool for 5 minutes. Turn oven temperature down to 150°C.
- Slice log across into fingers at 1-cm intervals, with a sharp serrated knife, using a gentle sawing motion.
- Place fingers on baking sheet and bake for 20 minutes, turning fingers over halfway through baking time. Remove from oven and cool thoroughly before storing in an airtight container.

To Prepare: **10 minutes** To Bake: **35 minutes** Makes: **about 20 pieces**

Phyllo sheets are less fattening than butter pastry and far easier to handle. Now, had I been Adam, Eve would've had to have done a bit better than just an apple. This pretty tart with its delicate, glass-brittle pastry and luscious custard filling, riddled with fragrant, juicy apples should have been Adam's undoing, instead of one miserable bite of a measly apple. Poor man!

Phyllo Apple and Almond Tart

Phyllo sheets 6, approximately 20-cm by 20-cm

Butter 2 Tbsp, melted

Heavy or double cream 175 ml (just under 1 cup)

Fine sugar 80 g (about ½ cup) or adjust to taste (I prefer it less sweet)

Eggs 2

Vanilla extract 2 tsp

Lemon juice 1 Tbsp

Salt a pinch

Almonds 100 g (about 1 cup, lightly packed), finely ground

Golden Delicious or Granny Smith apples 2, peeled, cored and sliced

Note : One 23-cm tart serves about 8 people.

- Set oven at 180°C.
- Lightly grease a 23-cm tart tin with melted butter. Lay a phyllo sheet in tart tin and gently mould it to shape of tin. Brush lightly but evenly with a little melted butter. Repeat process until all 6 skins are in place.
- Weigh down skins with 5 or 6 metal spoons criss-crossing each other. Bake for 8 minutes or until crisp and lightly golden. Remove from oven, remove spoons and set aside.
- In a large mixing bowl, combine cream, sugar, eggs, vanilla, lemon juice and salt and whisk lightly until well mixed. Stir in ground almonds.
- Lay the apple slices decoratively over base of tart shell. Stir egg and almond mixture and slowly pour over apples.
- Put tart into oven and bake for 30 minutes. Remove from oven and leave to cool slightly before slicing. Serve warm, as it is or with crème fraîche (page 159) or vanilla ice cream. Once tart is cold, cut with scissors if you want nice, neat wedges.

To Prepare: **15 minutes** To Bake: **40 minutes** Makes: **one 23-cm tart**

Billowy spoonfuls

Raspberries and white chocolate were made for each other. However, the relative and unexpected stridency of vodka adds a new element to this already luscious twosome and keeps things edgy and interesting. Get your mind out of the gutter; we're talking about dessert here! The fact that this doesn't use eggs means it's much easier and faster than a traditional mousse. A taste of this is almost certain to make any dessert lover purr with pleasure. *Rrrrrr*!

Raspberry, Vodka and White Chocolate Mousse

Regular white chocolate 175 g, broken into small chunks

Vodka 3–4 Tbsp

Fresh raspberries 100 g

Castor (superfine) sugar 1 levelled Tbsp (omit sugar if chocolate is very sweet)

Whipping cream 200 ml (about 1 cup), well chilled

Extra fresh raspberries sufficient to garnish

- Combine chocolate and vodka in a bowl. Put the bowl over a pot of water and bring water to a gentle simmer. Make sure bowl fits snugly over pot and don't allow water to get into the chocolate at any time.
- Meanwhile, process raspberries and sugar (if using) to a purée. Stir purée through a strainer to remove seeds. Discard seeds and set purée aside.
- When chocolate begins to melt, turn off heat but leave bowl over hot water. Stir chocolate until completely melted. Remove bowl from pot and set aside to cool slightly.
- Pour whipping cream into a large bowl and whisk until fluffy and standing in soft peaks. This should take about 2 minutes' worth of vigorous and continuous hand-whisking. Scrape cooled melted chocolate into whipped cream and fold in very gently until well-combined. Pour in raspberry purée and fold in lightly to achieve a streaked effect.
- Pour mousse into two large or four small glasses and chill to set until firm enough to support raspberries on top. Before serving, garnish each glass with a few whole raspberries.

heaven

To Prepare: 18 minutes **Serves:** 2–4

I love watching people get silly without even realising it, on alcohol-spiked desserts. This is one of my secret weapons. Excluding the traditional custard makes this less of a production and should give you more incentive to get up to mischief. It's liberally laced with bourbon but tastes so divinely innocuous, anyone eating this will never know what's hit them. This is so wickedly indulgent that I suggest skipping dinner, getting two spoons and spending a debauched evening in bed, wallowing in the pleasures of this sinfully sumptuous delight.

White Peach, Cherry and Bourbon Trifle

Fresh large white peach 1, skinned and cut into large cubes

Fresh dark cherries 100 g, ripe, firm, halved and pitted

Apricot jam or peach jam 1 Tbsp

Lemon juice 1 Tbsp

Southern Comfort (flavoured bourbon) 2 Tbsp + 100 ml (about ½ cup)

Shell-shaped madeleines 4, plain

Dark cherry jam 2 Tbsp

Mascarpone cheese 250 g

Castor (superfine) sugar (optional) 2 levelled Tbsp

Whipping cream 100 ml (about ½ cup)

Flaked almonds preferred amount, toasted, to garnish

- Put peach cubes, cherries, apricot or peach jam, lemon juice and 2 Tbsp bourbon into a pan. Cook for 2 minutes over medium heat or until liquids thicken and edges of the fruit soften. Do not overcook. Set aside to cool.
- Halve madeleines horizontally and sandwich together with cherry jam. Put madeleines into base of a 1-litre capacity glass bowl, about 15-cm across. Alternatively, put one madeleine each into 4 martini glasses and divide the remaining ingredients amongst the 4 glasses.
- Pour remaining Southern Comfort evenly over the madeleines. Spoon cooled fruit mixture over soaked madeleines.
- Put mascarpone and castor sugar into a large bowl and stir with a whisk until soft and creamy. In a separate and clean large bowl, whisk the whipping cream until it stands in soft peaks. Fold the cream into the softened mascarpone.
- Spoon the mascarpone and cream mixture over the fruit and cover completely. Refrigerate at least 4 hours. When ready to eat, garnish with toasted sliced almonds and serve.

To Prepare: **23 minutes** Serves: **2–4**

Cooking isn't just about following instructions. To really enjoy time spent in the kitchen, one needs knowledge beyond the boundaries of a recipe. Before knowledge comes curiosity, and if you're curious, you've come to the right place. Here, you'll find a goldmine of information on kitchen and food-related products and techniques, aimed at the inquiring and discriminating cook with a thirst for knowledge. So, get a cuppa, get comfy and go on, get out your reading glasses, no one's looking. You know, mothers and teachers are seldom wrong; knowledge *is* power!

Kitchen Smarts

Homemade Chicken Stock

I'm not above using instant liquid stock or granules but the good thing about making your own is you can control the fat and sodium content and avoid additives, if you have health concerns. At the end of the day, this doesn't take much effort and if you have the time, nothing beats homemade stock. This recipe makes about 4 litres. Simmered a bit longer and strained through fine muslin, it's good enough to serve as consommé.

Chicken bones 2 kg, with some meat on but no skin
Carrots 4, peeled and quartered
Celery 4 sticks, roughly chopped
Onions 3, large, peeled and quartered
Vegetable oil 2 Tbsp
Water 8 litres
Parsley 6 stalks
Dried bay leaves 2
Black peppercorns 1 levelled tsp
Sea salt (preferably Maldon sea salt) to taste

Note: This is a simplified version of chicken stock prepared in the classical French tradition. You can simplify it further by skipping the oven-roasting step and proceeding according to the recipe from there. The stock will still be tasty, though not as intensely flavoured or coloured. Stock made with roasted bones is called brown stock, and stock made with raw bones is called white stock. For white stock, omit vegetable oil from the recipe.

- Preheat oven to 220°C.
- Place chicken bones, carrot, celery and onion in a large roasting tin, pour oil evenly over everything and roast for about 45 minutes or until well-browned. Transfer to a stockpot or large saucepan with the water, parsley, bay leaves and peppercorns. Bring to the boil, then reduce heat and allow to simmer, uncovered.
- Skim off the scum and froth that rises to the surface with a spoon occasionally, to keep stock clear. Simmer for 2 hours or until the stock is very flavourful. Add enough salt to bring out the flavour. Do try to use a good-quality genuine sea salt; it makes a difference.
- Strain the stock through a very fine sieve or a muslin lined sieve. Allow to cool and remove any solidified fat from the surface.
- The stock will keep for up to 4 days in the fridge or almost indefinitely in the freezer. I like to freeze 500 ml (about 2–2½ cups) portions as this is the usual amount I use each time when cooking.

Homemade Crème Fraiche

You may have noticed crème fraîche mentioned throughout this book. Real crème fraîche is only made in French dairies in France. Crème fraîche is basically cream to which a culture has been added. The process imparts a tangy flavour to the cream and lengthens its keeping qualities. You can use it in place of sour cream for topping desserts and baked potatoes, or in cream soups and as a dip for chips or vegetable sticks. Seasoned to your liking, it also makes a marvellous salad dressing. My favourite use for it is over really rich chocolate desserts and fruit pies and tarts.

I've given up trying to find it in local supermarkets and for a while, resorted to using sour cream as a substitute, until I discovered this method of making it at home. Sour cream will do in a pinch but it lacks that distinctive airiness and tangy richness. Making it is not difficult at all. If you have ever made yoghurt at home, you will find making crème fraîche a breeze.

Heavy or double cream (at least 36% milk fat) 150 g (about 1 cup)
Full-fat plain, unsweetened yoghurt 50 g (about ⅓ cup)

Note: You can make any amount of crème fraîche. Just remember; you basically need 1 part yoghurt to 3 parts cream.

- Combine cream and yoghurt in a steel, plastic or glass container, or any container that doesn't react to acidic substances like yoghurt.
- Mix thoroughly with a clean dry spoon. Cover securely and leave to rest overnight or at least for 12 hours in a warm place.
- If your oven has a dough proofing feature, you could turn it on and leave the container in your closed oven. The temperature should not exceed 40°C. The top of your refrigerator would also work well.
- When the cream looks thick and slightly set, it's done. This should take no longer than 24 hours. If it does not set after 24 hours, it probably means the temperature was too high and the yogurt cultures (acidophilus) died or the temperature was too low and they were rendered inactive; in other words, they fell asleep before the job got done. If this happens, you'll have to chuck it out and start again!
- When done, refrigerate the cream immediately and use within 10–14 days.

The Best Coffee you can make at Home

My name is Denise and I am a coffee junkie and worse still, a purist junkie.

I have very strong views about our present-day coffee culture such as it has evolved. I'll keep them to myself. For anyone who holds the same views I do (you know who you are and stop pretending you're happy to pay $4.00 for a near thimble-sized shot of your daily caffeine fix) go get some decent coffee beans and we'll start the revolution right here!

Coffee in a Nutshell

Robusta The "lesser" and cheaper of the two main varieties. It's grown in all the major coffee producing regions of the world, and Brazil grows a lot of it. Indonesian Robusta is about the best and tastes mellower than Robusta beans grown anywhere else in the world. Much of Robusta beans that are grown go into the making of instant coffee.

Arabica The "greater" and more expensive (make that *much more* expensive) of the two. More refined and nuanced. Usually, with more acidity and less caffeine than Robusta. Also grown in all the major coffee producing regions, but usually grown at higher altitudes than Robusta. When buying coffee, look for "100% Arabica" on the label. There is a difference, and this difference is one worth paying for.

Terms You'll Need To Know

Body The weight of the liquid coffee in your mouth (think of it as the difference between light and dark soy sauce).

Acidity Sourness your tongue detects in a freshly-made cup–not the unpleasant tang even the best coffee develops when left standing. Most coffee begins to sour after about 20 minutes in the cup.

Aroma Refers to how pervasive and varied the smell of the coffee is after brewing. Coffee really is very much like wine; some are like single note symphonies, while others are highly complex and layered structures of different smells and flavours. Coffee is very often blended to achieve a pleasant balance of flavours and sometimes to make it cheaper (both to produce and to buy), again, much like wine. Premium coffee is usually left unblended.

My Favourite Single Origin or Unblended Coffees

Like wines, coffee beans are often named after the place they're grown, whether they're Robusta or Arabica. All the coffees I mention below are Arabica beans.

Guatemala Antigua Beautiful coffee. Floral, sometimes fruity, ever so slightly spicy, light to medium body, medium to high acidity.

Brazil Santos A very well-rounded, soft coffee. Nothing shocking or surprising for the coffee novice. Middle of the road, all the way. A very easy-going and agreeable coffee.

Sumatra Mandheling Luscious, low-acid, heavy-bodied, almost voluptuous. Sweet and earthy, with a distinct caramel flavour and a hint of spice. One of the most "heavy" coffees in the world.

Colombia Supremo Much in common with Brazil Santos, but more aromatic. If I had to live with one coffee for the rest of my life, this might be the one.

Kenya AA This is a coffee with a definite bite. High acidity, almost winey, berry-like flavours. A very distinctive, almost peppery and unforgettable aroma. It always reminds me of Shiraz somehow.

Toraja A very delicate coffee from Sulawesi, Indonesia, with a light to medium body, superb aroma, low acidity and a hint of nuttiness. It has an amazingly clean finish on the palate.

Equipment

Coffee grinder A worthwhile investment if you are particular about your coffee. Again, more hype about different grinds, and how a manual, hand-cranked grinder is far superior to an electric one. True as it may be, let's come down to earth and keep it real. An electric grinder gives you coffee good to go in seconds. A hand-cranked grinder takes quite a bit more time and muscle. The difference here is more coffee *aficionado* fantasy than reality. If there is a difference, it is so delicate and arcane that it eludes me. Freshly-ground coffee, even by electrical means, is definitely far superior to ready-ground coffee that's been waiting in transit for days and weeks or on the supermarket shelf for weeks and months, slowly but surely wafting off precious volatile oils and oxidizing in its vacuum packaging. Vacuum packing only delays oxidation, it doesn't prevent it.

Bottom line: buy beans and grind in small amounts as and when needed. Keep ground coffee in clean, airtight containers in the freezer. Keep your beans securely bound in their original packaging in the freezer. An important consideration is that you need different grinds for different methods. An espresso machine or *ibrik* (Turkish coffee pot) needs a very fine grind while a plunger pot requires a coarser grind so you don't end up with a murky, silty cup of coffee.

French press Also known as a cafetière or plunger pot, this is probably the best device for making good-quality coffee at home. It has the added advantages of being relatively cheap and easy to use and maintain. Keep it scrupulously clean. Take it apart and wash thoroughly after every use. You don't want residual coffee oils sticking to any part of it and turning rancid. This residue will perceptibly mar the taste and aroma of your next cup of coffee.

Water

The water for making coffee should be freshly drawn, very hot, hovering around 90°C, but not boiling. Some people use freshly-boiled bottled or distilled water. I use tap but if the quality of your local water is questionable, very hard or heavily chlorinated, then you might want to use bottled water. That covers everything you need to know to be able to savour really good coffee at home. Now, on to business.

Making Good Coffee

Put a kettle of freshly drawn water to boil. When water boils, fill your French press at least half-full, with boiling water. Wait a minute or so, then discard the water.

Put a heaping teaspoon or a levelled coffee scoop of medium ground Arabica coffee (origin or blend of your choice) for every cup (not mug) into the pot. Pour the requisite number of hot cups of water onto the ground coffee. Stir well, then put lid on (with the plunger extended out at full height). Leave to sit for about 3–4 minutes.

Push plunger gently all the way down. Pour out coffee, sweeten to taste and drink. Savour your coffee, but finish it before it has a chance to cool down, to get the best out of it. Don't reheat coffee; you'll kill it. Make in amounts that you can finish in one sitting. I don't add milk or cream to my coffee, ever. If you really want to, go ahead. **Cringe**. Sorry.

No scale…got cup?

I'd always had the habit of measuring baking ingredients by weight and I was for a long time, quite lost without my kitchen scale. That is, until out of the blue, my cakes began turning out hard, dry, cracked or poorly risen. It annoyed me no end and I almost stopped baking out of frustration. I thought I had lost my skill when in truth, my scale was damaged from years of constant use. I then realised how useful it is to know roughly how much a cup of flour, butter or sugar weighs, especially if you don't have a scale or yours has gone wonky. It's taken a while, but I can now bake very comfortably without a scale.

Measuring by cup is more convenient, but it's not a matter of merely dumping ingredients into the cup higgledy-piggledy. This is almost a science and involves principles of physics and meteorology. No, it's only half a jest. Although every manner and size of receptacle going by the name of "cup" has been called into service, I use a "standard" teacup with a capacity for holding, up to the brim, 200 ml of liquid.

Flour

It makes quite a bit of difference how you get the flour into the cup, and the difference stacks up with every cup. If your recipe calls for 3 cups of flour, for instance, different cup filling methods could mean a variance of between 300 g to 375 g. That's really quite a bit; 300 g will give a light and moist cake and 375 g with everything else remaining the same will likely yield a heavy and rather dry cake. So just how are you supposed to fill that 200 ml cup? There are 2 usual methods:

Dip and sweep Dip your cup into the flour container and scoop until cup is overflowing without banging or shaking it. Take a metal knife or spatula and sweep the edge across the top of the cup to remove excess flour without pressing down. There may be a slight variation of weight, depending on the moisture content of the flour (which can differ significantly). I don't recommend this method, as the flour might get compacted into the cup as you scoop it up and you may end up with more flour than you should use. By the dipping method:

1 standard cup flour =	125 g

Spoon and sweep Spoon the flour into your cup until heaping full. Do not pack down the flour, bang or shake the cup. Take your knife or spatula and sweep the edge across the top of the cup to remove excess, do not press down. Again there may be a slight variation depending on the moisture content and other factors like humidity and altitude. This is the method I use and it hasn't failed me yet. By the spooning method:

1 standard cup flour =	105 g

Some people sift flour before measuring or weighing but this step is not really necessary. Is it ever necessary then to sift flour? I only do so when I'm incorporating the flour into a very light mixture like whisked egg whites or a sponge mousse. Otherwise, I just whisk the dry flour in a large bowl together with raising agents, if using, to combine thoroughly, "aerate" and lighten it so it will mix evenly into the liquid ingredients without forming lumps or beads of unmixed flour or baking soda. The weights given are for plain (all-purpose) flour only as it is the most commonly used type in baking.

Butter

Measuring out butter is more straightforward than flour as there are no real variables. It's denser than flour, so a cup of it will weigh more than a cup of flour. To measure out butter, leave at room temperature until soft enough to scoop but still solid. Spoon into the cup, making sure you eliminate air spaces and level off the top with a knife as you would for flour.

1 standard cup butter =	150 g

Sugar

Sugar is also denser than flour and will usually weigh more than flour, cup for cup. It is porous (although less so than flour) and also subject to differing moisture levels. Like flour, it comes in quite a few variants and the difference in weight is quite significant. I have given the weight per cup of the most commonly used sugar varieties in baking. For sugar, whether you spoon it into the cup or dip the cup into the sugar container, the difference is not significant enough to affect the end result. You should, however, avoid compacting the sugar in the cup and again, you need to level off the top as you would for flour. Icing sugar should always be sifted before measuring as it tends to get compacted and form lumps. My measurements as follows:

1 standard cup sifted icing sugar =	90 g
1 standard cup castor (superfine) sugar =	160 g
1 standard cup fine granulated (white) sugar =	150 g
1 standard cup coarse granulated (white) sugar =	140 g
1 standard cup soft dark brown sugar =	120 g

Get Baking!

Using the information above, you'll be able to convert recipes quite easily. For instance:

200 g flour =	2 cups flour
200 g butter =	1⅓ cups butter
200 g castor (superfine) sugar =	1¼ cups castor (superfine) sugar

At the end of the day, you can't beat the scale for accuracy (unless it's faulty of course). On the other hand, who can resist the convenience of the cup? I know I can't. No more excuses, get baking.

Wine without Fear

These days, most people would probably know that a Shiraz or Syrah is red and a Chardonnay is white. All other assumptions aside then, I'll try to make this quick and painless, without insulting anyone or embarrassing myself. I'll start by admitting that I am not an oenophile, and my "qualifications" are unquenchable curiosity and a disturbingly long line of empty wine bottles behind me. My wine aspirations are to know as much as I can about wine so that I can drink as well as possible, for as far as possible, below $25 a bottle. As complicated as the subject of wine can be, it helps to remember that for all the hype, it really is just grape juice–make that very old grape juice. The only reason it ever came into being was because good clean, drinking water was hard to come by way back when, but people got to really like it so here it still is today.

Old World and New World Wines

Where in the world is wine produced? Most parts of Europe, notably France, Italy, Spain and Germany. Australia, New Zealand, the USA (notably California, Oregon and Washington), South Africa, Chile and Argentina. Old World wine are those from the original wine-producing countries of Europe, such as France, Italy, Spain, Portugal, Germany and Greece. New World wines come from everywhere else, like Australia, the USA, Canada, NZ, South Africa and Latin America.

France and Wine

It's difficult to ignore France's contributions to and influence on the wine industry. The French mapped the path and set the standard. They are also responsible for the mystique surrounding the subject of wine largely because of the system of Bordeaux wine classification which they came up with in 1855. We won't go deeper into that as it would only cloud the matter even more.

Prior to the emergence of varietal wines (wine labelled according to grape variety) which began around the 1970s, the French not only dominated the wine industry but practically monopolised it. The French rarely ever stated what grapes went into their wines. Rather than the grape variety, French wine labels usually stated the geographic origin of the wine, as location was deemed far more important than grape variety. They believed that above all else, "*terroir*" or the characteristics of the land (soil composition and climate) where the grapes were planted made the greatest impact on the finished wine. This belief perpetuated the notion of French winemaking mastery. Even Old World wines from other parts of Europe including Italy and Spain, were at best considered inferior or worse still, "cheap plonk". Consequently, French wines, especially if they were from Bordeaux, fetched very handsome and sometimes ridiculously high prices. The global consensus was that if it is French, it must be good; never mind what's in it. Thus, wine snobbery was born. However, there was a turn of events. At the Judgement of Paris in 1976 (a very bigwig wine tasting and judging event) for the very first time, in a blind tasting (the labels of the wine bottles were concealed) France was beaten in both red and white wine categories. The winners were a 1973 Chardonnay and a 1973 Cabernet Sauvignon, both from producers in the Napa Valley region of California. The judges were French. It was a monumental blow and a huge embarrassment to the French and marked the turning of the tide, in the global wine industry, towards New World varietal wines.

Reading the Label

Things to look out for in a wine label:

Grape Variety For example, Cabernet Sauvignon, Chardonnay, Sauvignon Blanc. This gives you an idea of the character of the wine, which will significantly depend on the character of the grape from which it is produced.

Place of Origin May be a country or a specific region of a country. Knowing the climatic conditions and winemaking traditions of its geographical origin can give a fair idea of the style of the wine.

Producer's Name or Bottler's Name May be one and the same or different. When a winemaker takes responsibility, from grape stage to bottled wines stage, you can usually expect a higher quality product.

Vintage The year the wine was produced, indicative of a quality-conscious producer and helps you gauge if a particular bottle is ready for drinking or should be laid down for further maturing.

Alcohol Content Normally ranges from 11–14.5 per cent. Lower alcohol indicates lighter body, and higher alcohol indicates fuller body. Also, wines from cooler climates tend to have a lower alcohol content, while those from warmer regions tend to have a higher alcohol content. Alcohol level is not indicative of quality; it only indicates how quickly the wine will go to your head.

Wine Components

Acidity Acidity is a component of a wine's character. It comes from the grape itself and helps to balance its overall flavour. It's present in both reds and whites, but tends to be more obvious in white wines, as the lower tannin levels allow acidity to come through more clearly. Acid in a wine will manifest itself as a prickle in your mouth, most notably along the sides of your tongue. The right amount of acid makes a wine lively and interesting; too much and it becomes "nervy" or "edgy"; too little and it seems flat and dull.

Body Body is the"weight" or feel of the wine in your mouth. Imagine the textural difference between weak tea and thick, creamy milk; that's what we're talking about. How does one determine the body of a wine? After you pour wine into a glass, hold it by the stem and swirl the wine around the inside of the glass, until it almost reaches the top of the glass. Then, hold the glass steadily up to the light, keep it still and look at the inside of the glass. You will notice that remnant streaks of wine are making their way down the glass into the wine at the bottom. These streaks are called "legs". The thicker these legs and the longer they take to drip down the side of the glass, the heavier the body of the wine. They indicate the viscosity or thickness of the wine, and usually the more viscous the wine, the higher the alcohol content as well.

Flavour and Aroma Flavours and aromas perceived in a wine can range from fruit, leather, earth, candy, spice and herb, even smouldering matches, to any combination of these and beyond. Additionally, traditional oak barrel fermentation and modern methods of "oaking" (adding oak chips to steel fermentation tanks) add flavours like butter, smoke, butterscotch, toast and vanilla, depending on the variety of oak used.

Tannin Tannin is a naturally occurring substance in the skins, seeds and stems of grapes. It provides structure, is almost absent in white wines, and is the reason that red wines keep much better than white wines. It has no "real" flavour or smell, but you will detect it as a drying, tightening sensation in the mouth and towards the back of your throat, with a faintly bitter aftertaste. Imagine biting into an unripe fruit or drinking really strong, unsweetened black tea–that unpleasant sensation is caused by the tannins present. It sounds almost nasty, but tannin is an essential component in red wines that are meant to age and develop character and complexity over time. Tannic wines like those from Bordeaux or Barolo are hard to swallow when young, but age incredibly well and mellow into sublime wines because of the generous tannins.

White Wine

The juices of both red and white grapes are actually almost similar in colour. So what is white wine? You take "white" wine grapes, extract the juice, filter the juice then put it in wooden barrels or steel tanks (more the case these days) and let it sit (fermentation) until it gets boozy.

How does it become boozy? The grapes are covered with naturally occurring yeasts from the atmosphere (that's right, the grapes aren't washed first! **Gasp**). These yeasts get into the juice, and when left to their own devices in the cosy confines of the barrels or steel vats, the yeasts start to feed on the natural sugars in the grape juice and produce alcohol in the process. *Ta-da*! Wine is born.

Some White Grape Varieties and The Wines They Produce

Chardonnay <sha-duh-nay> Dominant flavours and aromas are apple and vanilla for cool climate specimens, and pineapple, butterscotch and wood smoke for those from warmer climates, rich but acidic. Produces dry, pale golden wines; combined with Pinot Noir to make Champagne. In France, Chardonnay is usually labelled after the region whence it came, like Chablis, Montrachet, Pouilly-Fuisse. Elsewhere, it is labelled as Chardonnay. Chardonnay is unique, as unlike most other white wines, it is frequently fermented in oak barrels. The Australians in particular, love oak-fermented Chardonnay and many Australian Chardonnays will taste distinctly of buttery and toasty oak. However, more restrained and elegant Australian

Chardonnays are emerging with much less oak fermentation and sometimes, none at all.

Sauvignon Blanc <so-vee-nyoh/blahk> Dominant flavours and aromas of grass, gooseberries, figs, with a hint of asparagus. It has been said to smell like "cat pee". French examples are often described as flinty. Highly acidic, dry, aromatic and refreshing. This is the grape of the Loire Valley in France where it is used to produce Sancerre and Pouilly-Fume. Elsewhere, it's labelled as Sauvignon Blanc. Meant to be drunk young as it loses its piercing freshness and fades quickly. New Zealand is the most successful new world producer of Sauvignon Blanc, particularly Marlborough in South Island.

Semillon <sem-ee-yoh> Dominant flavours and aromas are green plums, figs and sometimes tobacco. Low in acid, full-bodied, almost "heavy", but still with a hint of citrus. Tends to produce alcoholic and sweet wines. Traditionally, it has been partnered with Sauvignon Blanc, particularly in Bordeaux, France to produce white Bordeaux. These two grapes complement each other, as Semillon adds voluptuousness to the blend, and Sauvignon Blanc lends some crackle and pop. The potential of Semillon as a varietal wine has never been fully exploited until recently. This underrated grape has been discredited for producing wines that are generally bland. The Australians, however, have raised its profile, especially producers in the Hunter Valley region who make complex, gorgeous, dry Semillons that age very well. Also produced in Washington, New Zealand and South Africa. The best way perhaps to enjoy this grape is to sample sweet white Bordeaux from Sauternes or Barsac. Look for "Sauternes" or "Barsac" on the label. These are dessert wines, meaning they usually accompany the dessert course.

Gewurztraminer <guh-vurts-trah-mee-ner> Dominant flavours and aromas of lychee, rose, sometimes red peppers and tropical fruit. Though considered a white grape, this variety actually has a pink skin. It produces wines that smell floral but taste dry. Alsace, in the northeast of France, produces the benchmark model for this style of wine. Alsace was once part of Germany which explains the "Germanic" style of Alsatian wines. Also produced as a varietal wine in Oregon, California, New Zealand, Canada and Italy. Oregon and New Zealand have had the most success with this variety. One of the few wines that seem made for Asian, and especially, Chinese food.

Riesling <reez-ling> Dominant flavours and aromas of citrus, apricots and honey; floral and relatively acidic. Prefers cool climates and reaches its zenith in Germany. Very versatile and capable of producing wines that range from honey-sweet to bone dry; has aging potential. Best examples are from Mosel in Germany, Alsace in France and Washington, USA. Dry Riesling is the other white wine that matches perfectly with Asian food.

Pinot Blanc <pee-no/blahk> Like a toned-down version of Chardonnay. Grown mainly in Alsace and also in Italy, where it is called Pinot Bianco and used mainly for sparkling wines.

Pinot Gris <pee-no/gree> Predominant peach flavour and aroma. Another pink-skinned, white grape variety. Hence the name *gris*, which means grey, referring to the less-than-white colour of the grapes. Again grown mainly in Alsace and also Italy, where it is called Pinot Grigio. Also grown in Germany, where it is called "Rulander", and Oregon. Generally makes rich, flavourful and quite alcoholic wines. Oregon is gaining a reputation for the quality of its Pinot Gris wines.

Chenin Blanc <sh-nair/blahk>
Dominant flavours and aromas of honey and green apples; highly acidic and crisp. Most famously used to make Vouvray and Saumur in the Loire Valley of France. Vouvray is frequently sweet, and Saumur is sparkling and dry. Even though Saumur is produced in the same way as Champagne, which is *methode champenoise*, by French law it cannot be labelled "Champagne" as it is produced outside of the Champagne region. Only sparkling white wine made from Chardonnay grapes in the Champagne region of France can legally be labelled as Champagne. Also makes a softer, gentler wine in California, labelled as Chenin Blanc. Popular in South Africa, where it is made into an even lighter, refreshing and slightly acidic wine commonly called Steen.

Red Wine

If all grape juice is basically the same colour, how then is red wine made? After squeezing the juice out, the solid matter comprising grape skins, seeds (pips) and some stems collectively known as "must" is added back to the juice. The grape must is rich in pigments and tannins. The pigments give colour and the tannins add astringency (some people call it character) and longevity to the finished wine. The two are then left to mingle until the juice darkens to the desired level. At this point, the juice is filtered and sent off for fermentation in barrels or steel vats, just as for white wine.

Some Red Grape Varieties and The Wines They Produce

Cabernet Sauvignon <cab-uh-nay/so-vee-nyoh>
Dominant flavours and aromas are blackcurrant and cedar. These grapes have relatively thick, dark skins and are highly tannic, producing astringent wines of deep colour and longevity. Quite undrinkable when young, but mellows beautifully with age, thus having great aging potential. Used to make Red Bordeaux in the Medoc, Graves, St Emillion and Pomerol regions of Bordeaux, France and Cabernet Sauvignon elsewhere, notably in Australia, California and Chile. French examples are drier and leaner while new world models tend to be fruitier, sometimes "jammy" and more alcoholic. The Maipo Valley vineyards in Chile consistently turn out impressive specimens –less tannic than French versions, less alcoholic and more elegant than most new world versions. Red Bordeaux is still considered the king of wines by connoisseurs.

Merlot <mer-loh> Dominant flavours and aromas of blackcurrant and dark berries. Like Cabernet Sauvignon but softer, fruitier and less tannic, because of the thinner skin of this variety. Used to make Bordeaux in France in combination with Cabernet Sauvignon and sometimes Cabernet Franc, depending on which area of Bordeaux we are talking about. In Graves and Medoc, cabernet dominates in the mix. In St Emillion and Pomerol merlot dominates. So, while Graves, Medoc, St Emillion and Pomerol are all examples of French Red Bordeaux, Graves and Medoc are leaner and more elegant because of the higher percentage of cabernet grapes. St Emillion and Pomerol will be slightly softer, fruitier and more rounded because the blends are predominantly merlot grape.

Also produced in Chile, California, Washington, Australia, New Zealand, Italy and South Africa. Chile and Washington have done very well with this grape variety.

Shiraz or Syrah <she-rahz>/<see-rah> Dominant flavours and aromas of blackcurrants, mulberries and spices, particularly black pepper. It originates from the Rhone Valley in France. In Australia, it is known as Shiraz. Its original name is Syrah and it says a lot about Australian wine producers, that "Shiraz" has overtaken the original name in familiarity among consumers. Produces rich, deep, dark and tannic wines capable of aging. The French model from the Northern Rhone is inky, tannic, peppery and extremely dry and when produced in the Southern Rhone region, is blended with with Grenache, a much softer, friendlier grape, resulting in a more approachable wine. The Australian model is quite different. In the hotter regions, it is generally very rich, full-bodied, almost syrupy but still quite tannic, with hardly any hint of spice, rather like alcoholic Ribena with a bite. Wines from the cooler regions like Victoria or Coonawarra, while sharing the same basic note of dark berries, are leaner and spicier.

Pinot Noir <pee-no/nwah> Dominant flavours and aromas of strawberries, raspberries and sometimes, beetroot. Rather sweet, thin-skinned and low in tannins. Produces wines that are generally light in both body and colour, with relatively low tannins, a distinct perfume and lots of character. Invariably compared with Bordeaux, and is both similar to and different. It has often been called the "feminine" equivalent of Bordeaux. Grown extensively in Burgundy, France, where it is labelled as Burgundy and also in Champagne, where it is used in combination with Chardonnay to produce Champagne. Pinot Noir is a notoriously fickle grape that prefers cooler climates. It is extremely variable and temperamental, but under the right conditions, it is capable of producing sublime wines that rival those of Bordeaux. Also grown in the cooler areas of California like Sonoma, and northern Oregon, New Zealand, Tasmania and Victoria in Australia, the cooler regions of Chile and South Africa. In Northern Italy, it is known as Pinot Nero.

Tempranillo <Tem-pra-nee-oh> Dominant flavours and aromas of strawberries, tobacco, vanilla and sometimes chocolate. Originates from Spain, where it is also known as Ull de Llebre and Tinto Fino, and is the country's most important grape. Used to produce Spain's most well known red wines, Rioja and Ribera Del Duero. The wines it makes are often favourably compared to Bordeaux and Burgundy. Personally, I think they have more in common with Burgundy and good Pinot Noir. Wines featuring Tempranillo are light to medium-bodied, with a gorgeous ruby tone; bursting with fruit, dry, but mellow, and able to age very gracefully. It is almost always oaked. Rioja, which is predominantly Tempranillo with some Garnacha, has amazing clarity in the glass and is as much a pleasure to look at as it is to drink. Traditionally, Rioja is constantly transferred from barrel to barrel during aging. This process prevents the formation of sediment and produces a wine of unusual clarity. Ribera del Duero is a recent entrant on the global wine stage. It is less distinguished than Rioja, but no less delightful and highly drinkable even when young, though it improves and mellows with bottle aging.

Nebbiolo <nair-bee-o-lo> Dominant flavours and aromas of truffles, tar, violets, roses, sometimes jasmine, and Asian herbs. There is a definite savoury aftertaste. This is a dark, thick- skinned, tannic grape. Grown primarily in Piedmont,

Northern Italy. Used to make Barolo and Barbaresco, famous wines named after areas in Piedmont, that are strong, tannic, dark and bursting with character. These wines can be overwhelming, though Barbaresco is the gentler of the two. When produced outside of Barbaresco or Barolo, even within Piedmont, these wines are labelled as Nebbiolo. Newer-styled wines are less tannic, are fruitier and much more approachable as compared to more traditional models. This grape seems to give its best only in Piedmont; wines produced elsewhere lack the signature intoxicating scent of the original. Complex and beguiling, with great aging potential; not a grape for the fainthearted.

Dolcetto<dol-chair-toe> Dominant strawberry flavour and aroma. Wines produced from these grapes are very fruity, light, dry, fresh and extremely drinkable. They are not made for aging and should be drunk within a year of the vintage. Italians drink this like it's water–with just about everything they eat.

Sangiovese <sahn-jio-vay-zee> Dominant flavours and aromas of cherries and truffles; the other great red grape of Italy, after Nebbiolo. Grown mainly in Tuscany and used to produce Chianti, Brunello di Montalcino and Vino Nobile di Montepulciano. Although present in all these wines, the Sangiovese grape presents itself quite differently in each case. Chianti is ruby-coloured, with hints of orange as it matures and acidic with a hint of bitterness. Brunello di Montalcino and Vino Nobile di Montepulciano are deep, dark wines with more substance and more aging potential. Many experts agree that Brunello di Montalcino is the Sangiovese grape's greatest achievement.

Malbec <mahl-beck> Dominant flavours and aromas of plums, dark berries and earth. Makes powerful, full-bodied, tannic wines of a startlingly deep violet colour. Originally from Bordeaux, France where it is mainly a blending grape. In France, the region of Cahors produces Malbec-dominant, and sometimes full Malbec wines, which are usually labelled as Cahors. Now widely planted and produced in Argentina. Argentine Malbec has more character and *oomph* than French specimens.

Zinfandel < zin-fahn-del>
Dominant flavours and aromas of blackberry, raspberry and pepper. This is California's very own grape, but it may have originated from Southern Italy. Made into both red and white wines, which actually look pale pink and are more like blush wines. This is actually a waste of the Zinfandel grape, which is capable of producing powerful, dry red wines worthy of aging and even sweet dessert wines, similar to port.

White Versus Red

The most important thing to know is that red wines keep (with the exception of Beaujolais Nouveau, other wines made from the Gamay grape and simple, easy drinking reds e.g. Lambrusco and rose wines), and white wines generally don't keep well (with the exception of some dessert wines). While reds improve over time, whites get flabby and dull. Red wines also contain much higher levels of polyphenols than white wines, owing to the higher concentration of pigments, and are consequently said to be a better choice for safeguarding cardiac health, when consumed in moderation, of course.

Storing Wine

Never, ever in the kitchen. Buying your wine, when you want to drink it, is best. If you have a wine chiller, put it somewhere relatively dark, preferably without too much vibration. One hour prior to serving, stand the bottle up to allow sediment to sink to the bottom. Do this only when you are ready to drink. Long-term storage should always be horizontal to prevent cork drying, wine oxidation and evaporation. When the bottle is lying down, the cork is in contact with the wine, keeping it moist and supple and thus less likely to break, crumble or shrink. When the cork shrinks, the space around the cork allows air to seep in and in time, the wine will become oxidised–you don't want this to happen! If you don't have a temperature-controlled wine chiller, keep your bottles horizontal in a dark, cool and vibration-free place, like your cupboard or the refrigerator if need be. Always keep your wines away from strong smells–smells seep in through the cork stopper. Generally speaking, avoid heat, fluctuating temperatures, light (natural and artificial), vertical storage (don't keep them upright) and vibration. Please: never, ever in the kitchen.

Serving Wine

The classic rule goes "serve white wine chilled" and "serve red wine at room temperature". The white wine rule is perfectly sensible, but the red wine dictum has caused me to be served virtually stewed wine, here in the tropics, at the requisite bloody "room temperature" more times than I want to remember. That rule originated from the temperate zone, and tropical "room temperature" is a very different beast from temperate "room temperature". The ideal serving temperature for red wine is 16–18°C. For white wine, a bit cooler. Just stick your red in the fridge for an hour before serving it to your guests. Chill white wines for about 2 hours prior to serving. When it comes to wine red or white, a little too cool is always better than a little too warm. And, uh, no ice cubes, please; they will melt and dilute the wine. If you're in a hurry, a bucket of icy water will chill a bottle in 30 minutes.

Wine Glasses

Wine glasses are generally thin, uncoloured and uncut, to allow you an unobscured view of the colour and consistency of the wine. If you want to have your wine in a teacup or disposable cup, the wine glass police will not come after you. But you should know that wine glasses are designed as such to enhance your wine drinking experience and heighten your awareness and appreciation of it through the senses of taste (thin rims), sight (clear glass), and smell (tapering bowl shape to direct aromas to your nose). The choice though, is entirely up to you.

White wine glasses have a slimmer base (bowl) and a longer, more elegant silhouette. The generally smaller capacity of a white wine glass allows you to finish your wine faster and get frequent top ups. This keeps the wine cool and fresh–the ideal way to drink white wine. When serving, fill the glass about ⅔ full.

Red wine glasses have a rounder, more bulbous base, and a larger capacity. Red wine is meant to sit around and linger in your glass, slowly revealing its character and nuances, layer by layer, bit by bit. The larger capacity of a red wine glass allows you to gently swirl your wine, and provides "breathing space" for the wine to develop its aromas and waft them up your nose as you drink. For red wine, fill the glass about ⅓ full.

Foods	Wines
Asparagus	Sauvignon Blanc (W), Very Dry Pinot Gris (W)
Asparagus with butter	Dry Chardonnay (W)
Avocado	Chardonnay (W), Chenin Blanc (W)
Creamy soups	Chardonnay (W), Pinot Gris (W), Australian Semillon (W)
Chicken in a creamy sauce	Chardonnay (W)
Oven roasted chicken	Chardonnay (W), Gamay (R)
Chilled, sharp, tomato-based soups or salads	Sauvignon Blanc (W)
Cured or smoked meats	Light Half Dry German Riesling (W)
Curry (especially fish curry)	The Driest Riesling (W)
Escargot	Pinot Noir (R)
Hot tomato-based soups	Chianti (R), Rhone Syrah (R)
Lentils with spices and/or tomatoes	Shiraz (R) Cabernet-Shiraz (R) Red Zinfandel
Marinated seafood or shellfish	Sauvignon Blanc (W), Dry German Riesling (W)
Mackerel	Dry Sherry
Mushrooms	Pinot Gris (W), Pinot Noir (R)
Oysters	Champagne, Very Dry Chardonnay (W) Chablis (W)
Paella	Young Rioja (R), Tempranillo (R), Pinot Gris (W)
Pasta in tomato sauce	Australian Shiraz (R), Sangiovese (R)
Pasta in creamy sauce	Chardonnay (W), Pinot Gris (W)
Pizza with tomato sauce	Dolcetto (R) Australian Shiraz (R)
Potato salad with mayonnaise	Sauvignon Blanc (W)
Potato salad with ham	Dry Riesling (W)
Quiche with asparagus or spinach	Sauvignon Blanc (W)
Quiche with ham or bacon	German Half Dry Riesling (W) or Alsace White
Roast beef, lamb or steak	Cabernet Sauvignon (R) Shiraz (R) Malbec (R)
Salad with citrus or vinegar-based dressing	Sauvignon Blanc(W) or Chenin Blanc (W)
Thai beef salad that's not too spicy	Half Dry Riesling (W) Australian Shiraz (R)

Appreciating Wine

This is a minefield if ever there was one. I do feel that this is highly subjective. Of course, some wine characteristics are universally appreciated. Fruitiness is always welcome, as is a long finish (a pleasant lingering after taste from the wine you have just drunk), or a pleasing balance of acidity and tannin. The subjective part is what we perceive in any given wine. I taste strawberry but you think raspberry, or I detect leather tones and you taste earthiness. I think I smell tobacco and you insist it's chocolate. You say lively and refreshing, but my mouth is puckering from the levels of acidity. No hard and fast rules again. Just because someone disagrees with you on a wine doesn't mean that you are wrong, or that the other person is right; it just means you both perceive differently. All I can say is taste, taste, taste, and then taste some more to develop your senses and appreciation. What more encouragement do you need?

Six To Start

You do generally get what you pay for, but once in a while you find a $10 bottle that tastes like $20. Once in a while, so don't get too hopeful. The following wines are some pleasant supermarket finds and some of my favourites. Most are comfortably priced.

Berri Estates Cabernet Sauvignon
Region: South Eastern Australia, Australia
Grape variety: Cabernet Sauvignon
Type: Red
Price: about $14.95
Tasting notes: Intense red fruit, primarily cherry and currants; full-bodied, almost heavy, with obvious oak; could do with a bit more acidity. If you like Ribena, you'll love this. All in all a very decent quaffing wine.

Paul Jaboulet Aine Cotes du Ventoux Les Traverses
Region: Cotes du Ventoux, Southern Rhone Valley, France
Grape variety: Grenache and Syrah
Type: Red
Price: about $23.95
Tasting notes: Inky garnet colour; subtle berry fruit flavours; very soft tannins; surprisingly, intensely savoury despite its light body; lifted by unexpected, but very refreshing acidity. Dry, but not abrasive; glides like silk down the throat. Elegant but approachable, with a satisfyingly long finish. Perfectly balanced and beautifully made. A steal at the price. I first tasted this 5 years after its vintage and it was perfect, although Southern Rhone wines are usually made for relatively early drinking.

Vina Albali Crianza Valdepenas
Region: Valdepenas, Spain
Grape variety: Tempranillo
Type: Red
Price: about $21.95
Tasting notes: Brilliant ruby hue; bursting with strawberry, chocolate, vanilla and tobacco flavours; hints of warm cinnamon and subtle tannins; medium- bodied and dry. Balanced acidity keeps smoke and spice elements in check. Extremely drinkable. I like this one a lot.

Gavi Terradavino Dolcetto d'Alba
Region: Alba, Piedmont Italy
Grape variety: Dolcetto
Type: Red
Price: about $24.90

Tasting notes: "Dolcetto" means little sweet one, but this wine is anything but sweet. It is Italy's everyday wine, and it should be. Fresh, vibrant purple-hued red; fruity as an orchard; dry and light-bodied, with lively acidity. Gorgeous with food, especially anything with garlic or tomatoes. You could very easily go through a bottle by yourself. The best quaffing wine I know.

Two Oceans Sauvignon Blanc
Region: Western Cape, South Africa
Grape variety: Sauvignon Blanc
Type: White
Price: about $24.30
Tasting Notes: Gooseberry, guava and a myriad of tropical fruit flavours; light straw colour with a green tinge; bracing and very welcome acidity; very clean, dry and fresh finish. Fantastic with Asian food, especially Thai. My favourite partner for spicy Asian food.

Grand Pavois Mauzac Sur Lie
Region: Limoux, Languedoc-Rousillon France
Grape variety: Mauzac
Type: White
Price: about $14.95
Tasting notes: This is a little-known wine outside of France, and is my favourite white wine for shellfish or just sipping. Light, very fresh, citrusy, with notes of green apple, peaches and just ripening banana; manages to remain bright and dry even in the presence of all those fruit flavours and in spite of being a relatively gentle wine. Definitely worth a try, especially at the price.

Really Bad Wine

In spite of continuing improvements in the wine industry, you may still stumble upon the occassional "off" bottle. If you open a bottle and are hit by an unpleasant, musty, mouldy smell, and the wine looks murky, you've got a "corked" bottle. This is a fault in winemaking and is caused by cork tainted with a fungus that can give rise to a chemical compound called 2, 4, 6–trichloranisole or TCA for short. Please do yourself a favour–return any such bottle and insist on a refund or a replacement. Any wine retailer, supplier or merchant worth his salt will gladly oblige. This information will go back to the producer or bottler. Do your bit to help improve standards–it's an ongoing process and knowing that any one of their bottles missed the mark is invaluable to winemakers who care about their product and are continually striving to improve. Fortunately, though cork is still very much in use, metal screw caps are increasingly popular and common. While some people have reservations about their ability to adequately seal a wine bottle for anything beyond immediate drinking, they do effectively wipe out the problem of corked wine and make broken corks a thing of the past.

Last Words

I'd like to finish as I started and remind you that we're talking about grape juice. To make an informed choice takes tireless reading, experimentation and probably a few disappointments. The global wine industry has made leaps, and it is now increasingly difficult to buy a poorly made bottle of wine, from anywhere at almost any price. Even supermarkets are getting increasingly savvy in matters, ranging from wine trends to storage and display. So the odds really are, increasingly, in your favour. It's no longer a question of buying a good wine, but more a matter of buying one you will like. Go forth then, and drink in good faith and to good health! Just remember, moderation in all things.